THE WORLD
OF GILBERT
AND SULLIVAN

Drawing by Youngman Carter

" A more humane Mikado never
Did in Japan exist."
[Darrell Fancourt as The Mikado]

THE WORLD
OF GILBERT
AND SULLIVAN

by

W. A. DARLINGTON

Illustrated

BOOKS FOR LIBRARIES PRESS
PLAINVIEW, NEW YORK

First published 1951 in Great Britain by Peter Nevill, Limited

Reprinted 1970 by arrangement with W. A. Darlington and his
literary agents, John Cushman Associates, Inc.

To my old friend and Fleet Street colleague,
A H GODWIN
who lent me his blitz-battered but serviceable
Gilbert and Sullivan library, and read my
proofs when my eyesight happened to be
temporarily inadequate to the task, I dedicate
the English edition of this book.

INTERNATIONAL STANDARD BOOK NUMBER:

0-8369-5573-0

LIBRARY OF CONGRESS CATALOG CARD NUMBER:

78-137372

PRINTED IN THE UNITED STATES OF AMERICA

CONTENTS

LIST OF ILLUSTRATIONS

Introduction

When I was a child of nine, I fell in love unreservedly and as it has turned out, irrevocably, with the theatre My family lived at that time in a remote part of Wales where the local theatre was an ill-appointed hall above a livery stable, which no actor with a care for his comfort could be persuaded to visit twice. A few road-weary straight plays limped in from time to time, but our main source of theatrical experience was musical comedy—tawdry, third-rate versions of not very recent London successes.

Knowing no better, we were satisfied. We bought the vocal scores of these fiascos and played and sang them till we had them by heart. My sisters—all three of them professional musicians in embryo—did full justice to the composers, and this disguised from us for a time the fact that the words of the songs were largely flapdoodle. For example, in *The Country Girl*, a very deservedly successful musical of those days, there was a popular sentimental love duet in which the hero and heroine called one another's attention to the cooing of doves. We sang this ditty with fervour, delighting in its sugary melody; and not till later, when the faculty for criticism had begun to dawn in me, did I realise the abysmal fatuity of the words we were singing. Here they are:

> Hark to that sound of coo-OO-oo
> > Of coo-oo-oo
> > Of coo,
> Calling to me and you-oo-oo
> > To me-ee-ee and you-oo
> Whether through darkest storms we go
> > Or under skies of blue
> > > Nothing shall sever
> > > I will be ever
> > > > True to my coo-oo-oo!

7

To those remote fastnesses such an organisation as the D'Oyly Carte Opera Company could not penetrate, and the names of Gilbert and Sullivan remained to us mere names, half apprehended as belonging to two men who had written some old musical shows, good enough in their time, no doubt, but now long out of date. Then, when I was away at school, a party of local amateurs put on *The Pirates of Penzance;* and I returned for my holidays to a family of Savoy opera fans who very quickly made a convert of me. I knew all the songs in *The Pirates* in a few days—no longer flat nonsense about people being true to their coo, but verses of humour and bite that were worth quoting apart from their music. I soon bought all Gilbert's works and revelled in them, swallowing them whole as a boy will; and when the family moved to London a year or two later, I, being eighteen, considered no time or money wasted which was spent in increasing my knowledge of the Gilbert and Sullivan repertoire. By the time I was twenty-five that knowledge was so complete that I believe an actor hardly could have said a wrong word or a musician have departed from Sullivan's harmonies in any of the best-known operas without my noticing the error.

Then, quite suddenly, Gilbert and Sullivan vanished out of my normal life. First I joined the Army in the First World War, and then I became dramatic critic on a London newspaper with a large musical staff who considered Savoy opera to be their business rather than mine. My youthful blind devotion to Gilbert also modified itself with increased experience, and I saw that his straight plays, which I had once thought unjustly neglected, had found their proper level on the shelf where they now accumulate dust. I realised without indignation that some critics whose judgment I respected found Gilbert verbose, tiresome, and slow not only in the straight plays, which I no longer cared for, but also in the libretti which I still considered the quintessence of their

8

kind. In fact, I got Gilbert into proportion—and found that I still admired him, this side of idolatry. But the years passed and I never had the chance to say so in print.

Unexpectedly, the chance came. An American publisher noticed that with the passing of the years the popularity of the Gilbert and Sullivan operas in the United States was growing rather than waning, and realised that to a very large percentage of American playgoers Gilbert's share of the collaboration must be obscure if not unintelligible. Not only the local and topical allusions of the texts, but the whole social and political background against which they had been written, must be alien and remote affairs to the new Savoy devotees of to-day He looked about him for an English author who might write him a book in which those allusions should be explained and that background recreated; with the result that I was rung up one day and asked if the idea of such a book appealed to me. I answered at once that it appealed to me very strongly indeed, and was shortly afterwards told to go ahead and write it.

I sat down to my task, then, in the belief that I was writing exclusively for an American public, since the explanations that I was about to make would (I thought) be so familiar to English readers that they would seem trite and unnecessary. As soon as I came to grips with my subject this belief began to fade. Even though the goods I was producing were intended for export only, they seemed perfectly suitable for the home market, too. The world of which I was writing, the complacent Victorian world in which Gilbert and Sullivan lived, had had its last vestiges blown into nothingness in 1914, and few British playgoers much under fifty years of age could have any significant memories of its values. Perhaps, after all, the book that I was writing might find a place on English bookshelves with a little revision.

That revision has been done. I have also taken the opportunity to correct a few mistakes and oversights which I had allowed to creep past me into the American edition; but even so it is with diffidence that I see this book go out to take its chance with that frighteningly erudite body, the Gilbert and Sullivan public in this country. That public knows so much, and knows it so thoroughly, about Gilbert's text and Sullivan's music. It is steeped, as I was once but can never be again, in Gilbert and Sullivan lore of every kind; and I am only too conscious that the final proofs of the book as I pass them irrevocably to the printer, may contain much evidence that I no longer have the operas by heart.

In order to avoid major errors I went to a fountain-head of wisdom on this particular subject; I obtained from Mr. D. Graham Davis, the editor of the *Gilbert and Sullivan Journal,* a list of any failures in knowledge or accuracy which he noticed when he read the original American edition. I received that list with trepidation, but read it with some relief —it was not as formidable as I had feared. I want to express here my sincere gratitude to Mr. Davis for having made it, more especially as it enables me to answer in advance one point which otherwise might crop up again. Mr. Davis noted several references which combined to show that in writing my book I had used a very early Gilbert text. He made no adverse comment, but the implication is that he thinks it is a pity that I did not get hold of a more up-to-date edition. I do not quite agree. I used the only text that I could conveniently get hold of, the ordinary published series of Gilbert's plays. I used this because it never occurred to me not to; though I knew, of course, that in some ways Gilbert's printed texts had been modified in stage practice. If the question had not been raised, I should never have given it a thought. But since it has been raised, and since a point which has occurred to Mr. Davis may well occur to other Gilbertian scholars, let me take this opportunity of saying that as I am mainly dealing in this book with the libretti not as they are seen on the stage of to-day but as they emerged from Gilbert's mind many years ago, the original text is the proper one for me to use. And anyhow, my edition is dated 1910; and I feel that what was good enough for Gilbert a year before he died might well be good enough for me now.

The fact is that textual niceties are not within the scope of a book such as this, and while I have tried to be accurate I have deliberately avoided the scholastic approach to Gilbert. When I was a schoolboy I read the Greek comedies of Aristophanes and the Latin comedies of Plautus and Terence under an erudite old gentleman who was more at home in the languages of these authors than in his own, and who explained their witty sallies to his class with appreciative chuckles while we yawned behind our hands till our jaws were in danger of dislocation. At about the same time another enthusiast interpreted to us the humorous niceties of such Shakespearean characters as Launcelot Gobbo, with similar result. I am grateful now to these pedagogues for driving into my unwilling memory a certain useful groundwork of knowledge, but I was not then and am not now of their kidney. I am a practical man of the theatre who knows that a joke that has to be explained is dead so far as the stage is concerned, that the only joke which has any value there is the one that causes an audience to laugh spontaneously, and that an audience can laugh spontaneously only at things that it can instantly understand. If I make any explanations of obscure passages in Gilbert's text, they are therefore purely incidental—my main aim is not to fiddle about with detail but to help modern audiences to an easier approach to Gilbert's work as a whole.

Anyhow, why should we allow Gilbert's occasional obscurities to trouble us, seeing that he never did so himself? Often he set himself technical problems so difficult that even

11

he, master of his craft as he was, could not solve them completely. Take, for example, the duet between Captain Corcoran and Little Buttercup in the second act of *H.M.S. Pinafore*, which begins " Things are seldom what they seem." Almost every line in this lyric is intended to suggest some proverb or parable to the mind, and at one point the scheme calls for the quick-fire effect of four consecutive rhyming lines. Here are the four lines in question, in the second verse:

> Paw of cat the chestnut snatches;
> Worn-out garments show new patches;
> Only count the chick that hatches;
> Men are grown-up catchy-catchies.*

The first three lines are clear enough. The story of the monkey who used the cat's paw to pull chestnuts out of the fire is well embedded in our collective memory. The warning not to patch old garments with new cloth comes in the Bible. " Don't count your chickens before they are hatched " is one of the most familiar of our proverbs. But what is this fourth line, to which Gilbert has had to have recourse to get his difficult fourth rhyme? Presumably, at the moment when he wrote it, Gilbert hoped that it would convey some sort of meaning, but plainly he could not have cared much whether it did or not, or he would have clarified it. And if he did not care, neither need we. We know what the song means, and on the stage that is all that matters.

One more point. Inevitably, by its terms of reference, this book deals with words rather than music; Gilbert must therefore be its central character, with Sullivan playing a

---

* A reader has elucidated this. In his youth, he says, he remembers mothers and nurses pretending to throw their children into the air and to catch them again, saying or singing " catchy-catchy " as they did so. Gilbert's meaning, therefore, for those who can take it, is " Men are grown-up babies "; or in proverb form, " The child is father to the man."

minor, almost an incidental, part. From this it has been assumed in some quarters that I regard Gilbert as the greater man of the two. As this is not quite what I think, I am taking this chance of elucidating the matter.

If the two men are considered separately, I feel no doubt that Sullivan's talents were of a higher order than Gilbert's. Separately, however, neither man produced works of genius, whereas in collaboration they frequently did. And in that collaboration, because he had the stronger character of the two, and was more at home in the theatre and knew more clearly what he was doing, Gilbert took the lead. This does not make him in my eyes the greater man; but it does make him much the more interesting.

CHAPTER I

Gilbert and Sullivan For Ever?

If William Schwenk Gilbert and Arthur Seymour Sullivan still exist on an astral plane in any form which enables them to see what is going on on earth, they must be two of the most astonished ghosts in all the shadowy realms.

Sullivan's is likely to be the more surprised spirit of the two, for he died in 1900 with the bitter taste of defeat upon his lips. He had nót, so he thought, done his best work, and almost all the work he had done was doomed to swift oblivion. Living as he had in that most serious-minded age in all his country's history, the second half of the nineteenth century, he had been told again and again by severe critics in solemn journals that he owed it to his genius and to his position in society to write serious music. He was told, and he firmly believed, that in spending so much of his best years writing lucrative but flimsy and short-lived stuff like comic opera he was prostituting his art.

More grand operas like his *Ivanhoe,* more oratorios like his *The Golden Legend,* that is what he should have done to make his name known to posterity—so his critics said. But grand opera and oratorio do not make great fortunes for their composers, and Sullivan had expensive tastes. He liked to gamble at Monte Carlo, and this was a very expensive taste indeed; for though there are many stories of his presence at the tables there is no record that he ever came away from them a winner. Also he liked associating with crowned heads and giving birthday presents to royal princesses. In fact, he needed money in very large quantities, and could get it only by continuing to degrade himself.

14

Also, he died at a time—perhaps the only time since his partnership with Gilbert began—when it seemed that the Savoy operas were done with. Four years before, in 1896, the last of the series, *The Grand Duke*, had failed to please the public. Three years before that, in 1893, the last but one, *Utopia, Limited*, had run for a mere 245 performances. His only excuse for writing light music had failed him, and there can be little doubt that he died believing that he had been false to his trust as an artist. It is true that one serious musician at least, Ethel Smyth, told him firmly that his masterpiece was not *The Golden Legend* but *The Mikado*: but he had been neither pleased nor persuaded by her verdict.

Gilbert, the elder of the two men but much the healthier—for Sullivan was liable all his working life to fierce bouts of illness—lived until 1911 and saw the development of Gilbert and Sullivan opera from an outstandingly successful theatrical achievement into a craze, almost a cult. By the time he died the D'Oyly Carte Opera Company had become a permanent institution, on the road from year's beginning to year's end, and received everywhere with a delight that bordered on hysteria. When it visited Oxford or Cambridge, for instance, young men from the Universities would rise at dawn and stand patiently in queues for five or six hours to make sure of tickets for themselves and their friends. Gilbert knew before he died that Sullivan and he had built more permanently than they or anybody could have hoped, but still I think he must be surprised if he knows just how well their frail-looking edifice has lasted.

For I believe it is true to say that never in the history of the theatres of the world has there been anything to match the continued popularity of Gilbert and Sullivan opera. It is the common fate of entertainments which have been specially popular with their own generation of playgoers to fall specially deeply out of favour with the next. Musical shows in particular go swiftly out of fashion; their music lingers on, but the shows themselves are forgotten, and seldom bear revival. Yet from the time, now more than 70 years ago, when the first Gilbert and Sullivan composition was seen and heard in London, there has hardly been a moment when a D'Oyly Carte Opera Company has not been playing one or other of the operas. Certainly there has never been a generation of playgoers (and a new generation of playgoers arrives every seven years or so) which has shown any sign of thinking that the operas ought to be put on the shelf. London and New York may have appeared to think so at times, only to find out each time that they were wrong. Country audiences, less fickle-minded than the city sophisticates, and not so firmly wedded to novelty, have never wavered in their enthusiasm.

There must be a reason for such a phenomenon, and quite a number of people seem to think they know what it is. Unfortunately, they do not all agree on the point, which therefore remains unsettled. Some say that it is the unique quality of tunefulness in Sullivan's music, which keeps so fresh and alive that it is able to drag along with it the dead weight of Gilbert's outmoded humour. Others say that it is the words of the songs that matter—that while much of Gilbert's dialogue is stale and verbose and unfunny, his lyrics have imperishable quality, and give distinction to Sullivan's music, which would not otherwise have survived— and has not survived when set to other men's verses.

People who argue in either of these ways seem to me to forget certain very solid facts. When the two men met, Gilbert was 41 and Sullivan 35, and both were already eminent in their professions. Gilbert was a dramatist with a number of straight plays to his credit and a reputation for an odd kind of topsy-turvy humour peculiar to himself, which came out in his comedies but was seen at its best in the verses he wrote for a weekly paper called *Fun*. He was known to have an ambition to write serious comedy. Sullivan was a prolific song-writer, and was regarded as the most promising composer in the country. The work that they did together consists of thirteen operas* and was spread over 19 years, during which each of them was free for a great deal of his time to pursue his own separate career. Yet nothing that either man did by himself has had the lasting quality of their joint compositions. Nobody to-day stages Gilbert's straight plays or Sullivan's grand opera. These were works of talent which belonged to their own time, and have perished. Gilbert-and-Sullivan is the work of genius, and has so far proved imperishable. It follows from this that all talk of which partner contributed most to the collaboration, or which is the more responsible for its continued vitality, is utterly futile— as futile as a discussion which of two parents could do most without the other towards bringing a child to birth.

This comparison with a married couple is inevitable, and bears very close scrutiny. The most detached and objective of all the biographers who have written about the two men is Hesketh Pearson, and he makes the point that while the differences between their characters and outlook made it impossible for them to be friends (to the end of their lives they did not like each other well enough to call each other by their Christian names), Sullivan, if he had been a woman, would have made Gilbert a very suitable wife. The analogy is very clear when we look at their artistic relationship, for it was always from Gilbert that the first impulse came. He worked out the plot of his story in full detail before he began upon the lyrics, and not until the lyrics were in his hands did Sullivan begin to compose the music. And although Sullivan was constantly yearning to get away from the necessity of following where Gilbert's verses led him, the fact is now clear that it was under that very necessity that his best music was written.

* Excluding the early work, *Thespis.*

17

It was Sullivan's restiveness, his longing to express himself (as he saw it) more fully in his music, that caused the partners to separate in the end; and here, too, the analogy with a married couple holds good. To read the correspondence between them, to hear Sullivan constantly asking for more scope and Gilbert firmly insisting that they must go on doing what they do so very well, is to think of an ambitious wife pining to go into high society and cut a dash while her wise husband points out that while they are important people in their own town, in high society they will run the risk of being nobodies.

It is well that Gilbert's importance to the partnership should be heavily stressed, for two reasons. One is that nobody realised it at the time—not even Carte or Sullivan, who should have been the first to acknowledge it. As I shall go on to show in later chapters, Gilbert, who, like the sun and Yum-Yum, really knew his worth, constantly found himself galled by their lack of appreciation. They paid lip-service to his talents, no doubt, in order to keep the peace; but in times of stress it became evident again and again that they both resented having to follow where he led, and both secretly agreed to the general public's view, that in any kind of opera the composer is all-important and the man who writes the words hardly matters.

Till quite recently there was a legend, everywhere accepted as fact, that when a command performance of *The Gondoliers* was given before Queen Victoria at Windsor Castle, Gilbert's name was omitted from the programme. Hesketh Pearson accepts this story as gospel, and adds a piece of picturesque detail that while Gilbert did not score a mention, " the name of the wig-maker was printed in bold type." This is not quite accurate. What really happened, I learn from another authority, was that both collaborators were given proper credit on the programme; but that the Court Circular, in its subsequent account of the proceedings, referred to *The Gondoliers* as " Sir Arthur Sullivan's comic opera," and then, in reproducing the programme, left out both composer and librettist but included the wig-maker.

This takes much of the colour out of the story, and I am sorry for it. Like many other myths, it had an essential artistic rightness and ought to be true. It reflected what Queen Victoria thought about the comparative importance of words and music, even if she did not take this drastic way of saying so. She knew a good deal about music, and she took a personal share in persuading Sullivan that he ought to be writing grand opera. With no sense of humour at all, and an immense conception of the sanctity of royalty, she must have regarded the irreverent Gilbert as a thoroughly bad influence on her admired composer. It is safe to guess that when she gave Sullivan his knighthood, the idea that his partner could possibly be worthy of a similar honour never for one moment crossed her mind.

The other reason for laying particular emphasis on Gilbert's work is the likelihood—the possibility, anyhow—that here we have the chief reason why the Savoy operas have lived longer than others of their kind. In the operatic world it is unheard of, as Sullivan was fond of pointing out, for the librettist to be as important as the composer; and it may be that Gilbert, by altering the usual balance of power, made possible an unusual success.

Words written to music can never have much literary merit or wit, but music written to words may—as Sullivan so often showed—not only bring out the wit of the words but be witty itself as well. That is exactly where Gilbert and Sullivan differs from other compositions supposed to be of the same kind, that you remember not only the melodies but the words, and are not satisfied unless you can recapture them both.

Gilbert and Sullivan

During one of the quarrels which finally broke the collaboration, Sullivan let it be seen that he thought he had been effacing himself in favour of his librettist for a dozen years, and that he felt it was time that the librettist effaced himself for a change. Gilbert, always the more realistic of the two, put him right by pointing out that each was an expert in his own part of the work, and that if they met it must be as master and master, and not as master and slave. Because Gilbert was a master, perhaps as great a master as has ever lived, of the art of writing verses to be set to music, the songs that he wrote are as fresh and alive as the music to which Sullivan set them. One of the chief proofs of the " settable " quality of Gilbert's lyrics is the way in which Sullivan was able to pull them about, or vary the rhythm.

A single example will be enough to show what I mean. In *The Gondoliers*, at the end of the first act, Gianetta and Tessa have a verse each of a song of farewell to Marco and Giuseppe. Gianetta begins:—

> Now, Marco déar,
> My wishés héar:
>   While you're away
> It's understóod
> You will be góod
>   And not too gay . . .

She sings her verse with the stresses on the last word of the line, as Gilbert wrote them. Then Tessa follows; but in writing her verse Sullivan has achieved a subtle variation by throwing the stress back, away from the rhyming word to the middle of each line:—

> You'll láy your head
> Upón your bed
>   At sét of sun.
> You wíll not sing
> Of ánything
>   To ányone . . .

20

The whole verse sounds as if it were written in quite a different metre. The idea is most ingenious, and the effect is simple and charming. Resourceful Sullivan!—but he would not have been able to do that kind of thing with the lame verses of a lesser lyric-writer. In that way, Gilbert was unsurpassable. His verse had an elasticity for which Sullivan must have been thankful a thousand times.

A further point to be noticed about Gilbert's lyrics is that very few of them have gone out of date. There is, of course, one type of song, at least one example to every opera, of which the whole point is topical allusion and contemporary satire, and these naturally began to be old-fashioned almost as soon as they were written. Ko-Ko's song, " I've got a little list," in *The Mikado,* and the Mikado's own song about letting the punishment fit the crime are obvious examples. The Sentry's song in *Iolanthe,* with its calm assumption that everybody is either Liberal or Conservative, sounds oddly in the ears of Englishmen in whose Parliament the Socialist Party may have a majority and Liberals are only a handful. The Colonel's song, " A heavy dragoon," in *Patience,* is crammed full of topical and literary allusions which only a research student can understand to-day without an encyclopædia. But such songs are fairly rare, and the average audience is quite ready to be indulgent about them.

In the great mass of the songs and concerted numbers, however, there are no topical allusions at all. Either they express some idea arising out of the plot, or they carry on the plot itself. This gives them a dramatic as well as a musical interest, so that they can go out of date only when the opera itself ceases to appeal.

The two first solos in *The Mikado* give clear examples. As soon as the opening chorus is over, in which the Gentlemen of Japan introduce themselves, Nanki-Poo enters and asks for Yum-Yum. One of the nobles says, " But who are you, who ask this question?" and Nanki-Poo tells them in the song " A Wandering Minstrel I," in which Gilbert gives Sullivan the chance to write spirited parodies of three different kinds of popular melody—a sentimental ballad, a song of the sea, and a patriotic ditty. Nothing is more admirable in Gilbert's writing, it may be remarked in passing, than his quickness off the mark. Having established Nanki-Poo, he now sketches the main situation of the opera in a short passage of dialogue, and then gives Pish-Tush a song in which he explains the whole complicated situation of Ko-Ko's release from prison and his appointment to the post of Lord High Executioner.

The first verse of this song shows how the Mikado decreed that anybody who flirted should be beheaded. The second describes the consternation which the decree caused. Here is the third : —

> And so we straight let out on bail
> A convict from the county jail
>   Whose head was next
>   On some pretext
> Condemnèd to be mown off,
> And made *him* Headsman, for we said
> " Who's next to be decapited
> Cannot cut off another's head
>   Until he's cut his own off."

In that one song we can see all the basic qualities which make Gilbert and Sullivan different from all other light musical shows. The audience have to hear the words of that song, for if they don't they will miss an important development of the story. Since every word had to be listened to, Sullivan had to set it so that every syllable was brought out clearly (which was the real reason for Sullivan's recurrent discontent), and it had to be given to a singer with a singularly clear enunciation. Pish-Tush is not an important character, for this is his only song; so it follows again that the whole company, down to the least considerable member of the chorus, had to be unusually articulate.

The lyrics, then, still remain for the most part fresh. It is in the spoken dialogue that Gilbert's work shows signs of fading away in patches. Every here and there are passages which seem no longer in the least funny even to the sincerest of Gilbert's admirers. For instance, in *The Pirates of Penzance* occurs this dialogue between the Pirate King and Major-General Stanley:—

Gen. I ask you, have you ever known what it is to be an orphan?

King. Often!

Gen. Yes, orphan. Have you ever known what it is to be one?

King. I say, often.

Gen. I don't think we quite understand one another. I ask you, have you ever known what it is to be an orphan, and you say " orphan." As I understand you, you are merely repeating the word " orphan " to show that you understand me.

King. I didn't repeat the word often.

Gen. Pardon me, you did indeed.

King. I only repeated it once.

Gen. True, but you repeated it.

King. But not often.

Gen. Stop, I think I see where we are getting confused. When you said " orphan," did you mean " orphan "—a person who has lost his parents, or often—frequently?

King. Ah, I beg your pardon, I see what you mean—frequently.

Gen. Ah, you said often—frequently.

King. No, only once.

Gen. (*irritated*) Exactly, you said often, frequently, only once.

That passage was written for a generation which had a childish delight in puns, a form of humour now thought crude. Also, it depends for its point on the fact that in those days the word " often " was regularly and properly pronounced " orf'n " so that the pun was an exact one. Nowadays a great many people pronounce " often " as it is spelt, and for them the pun does not exist. There must be many other people beside the General who are irritated by the time that passage is over. Yet even so it is necessary to the plot.

How much, I wonder, do such patches of decay matter to the fabric of the various operas? As it happens, I have a personal experience to draw on which helps to answer this question. About 1925, being then comparatively young to my job of dramatic critic, I was invited by the Gilbert and Sullivan Society to take the unpopular end in a debate at the Society's headquarters. I was asked to put the case that Gilbert's libretti were going out of date to such an extent that they would have to be re-written if the operas were to have any hope of surviving much longer.

The Gilbert and Sullivan Society, as you may imagine, consists very largely of enthusiasts and devotees who consider that every word or note written by the two Masters is sacrosanct. My chairman on that occasion was Sir Ernest Wild, the Recorder of London, a distinguished lawyer, who began the proceedings in true *Trial By Jury* manner by saying that his mind was free from bias of every kind, but how anybody could have the impudence to come before the Society and talk such vile heresy as I was obviously going to talk, he could not imagine. And what Sir Ernest said in jest was obviously the serious opinion of some of the fanatics in the body of the hall. It was rather like arguing at Salt

Lake City before Brigham Young in favour of monogamy, or at Moscow before Stalin in favour of private enterprise.

Anyhow, I made one convert—myself. By the time I had finished putting my case I really did believe that Gilbert and Sullivan opera was doomed to swift oblivion if Gilbert's dialogue was not carefully rewritten, the topical references in the songs amended, and drastic cuts made. There was, of course, a smashing majority against me; and when I had recovered from the heat of the debate I hoped that the majority would prove right and I wrong, for I knew well enough that you cannot tinker with masterpieces without losing more than you can possibly gain.

Time has proved me wrong. The operas still go unchanged on their triumphant course, and still make devotees in each generation of young playgoers as it comes along. The Gilbert and Sullivan Society has forgiven me my ancient blasphemy and has made me one of its Vice-Presidents. And here I sit, by the irony of fate, writing a book for which there would have been no need if I had been right all those years ago. For one part at least of my prophecy has come true. In 1925 even comparatively young playgoers, such as I then was myself, were familiar with the social and political background against which the operas were set. If we had not ourselves grown up against the same background, our parents had. From the books on their shelves, the photographs in their albums, the stories on their lips, we were as much at home in that setting as in our own. Now, more than a quarter of a century later, that is no longer so. Even in England, the manners and customs, the beliefs and the fancies, the whole civilisation of the 70's, 80's and 90's of the last century are remote and strange to the present generation. In America, new discoverers of the operas have the added disadvantage of remoteness not only in time but in space.

Most of Gilbert's humour is still funny, because it is based on fundamentals. His power of mock solemnity, as exemplified in the scene where Major-General Stanley, having got his puns out of his system, throws himself on the mercy of the pirates on the plea that he is an orphan boy, or in that other scene in the same opera where the policemen put up a terrific martial chorus about going " forward on the foe " but don't in fact move a step till they have to—this is uncorroded by time. So is his own particular brand of humour, which has added the word " Gilbertian " to our language, and consists of sticking to logic in the face of plain fact.

An example of this was seen in Pish-Tush's song, quoted above. " We made him Headsman, for we said ' Who's next to be decapited cannot cut off another's head until he's cut his own off.' " Though in fact this idea wouldn't work out for a minute, logically it is quite incontrovertible, and on it Gilbert bases all the topsy-turvy incidents of the opera generally accounted his best. Here is fabric which hardly yields at all to time.

But between the true Gilbertian humour which will always be funny and the purely verbal quips which will never be funny again, there is a great deal of running commentary on life as it was lived in Gilbert's own time which is funny or not according to one's own knowledge of those times, or lack of it. Just as one's enjoyment of Shakespeare's plays grows with our knowledge of the Elizabethan way of life and Elizabethan English, so a little knowledge of the England in which Gilbert and Sullivan worked may give point to many an allusion which must otherwise be incomprehensible. And so I propose in this book to look through the operas in the light of what knowledge I have, and to restore the background where it seems to have faded so badly that the young Gilbert and Sullivan " fans " of to-day cannot be expected to make out the pattern.

CHAPTER II

Gilbert as Pioneer

Before I go on to fill in, as best I may, the social or political
background against which each opera was seen and understood in its own time, I must give some account of the theatre
in which Gilbert and Sullivan, but especially Gilbert, had to
work. I say " especially Gilbert " because he was by
temperament and choice a man of the theatre, who had
always meant to work for the stage, and had written fifteen
plays by the time he was twenty-four; whereas Sullivan came
into the theatre almost by accident, and, as we have seen
already, made constant though abortive efforts to leave it
again.

Gilbert first worked with Sullivan in 1871, and it was in
that very same year that a little-known actor named Henry
Irving drew all London to see him at the Lyceum Theatre in
a play called *The Bells*. That was certainly a historic year
in the annals of the British stage; and when one considers
further that it was in that same year that the dramatist T. W.
Robertson died—the famous Tom Robertson who had
revolutionised stage practice and paved the way for the
modern realistic dramatists with his " cup-and-saucer
comedies "—one gets the impression that a great theatrical
period was in being.

Nothing of the sort, however. The London stage for
which Gilbert began to write, and on which he first tasted
success in 1866 with a short piece called *Dulcamara,* was an
actor's stage entirely. Its dramatists were hack writers with
no ideas of their own, whose only claim to attention was the
technical skill with which they could furbish up adaptations
from the French.

27

An outstanding example of this kind of dramatist was Dion Boucicault, whose name is still held in high honour wherever theatrical traditions are cherished. He was an actor, and his plays in consequence were extremely actable, but as writing they were quite terrible. In 1855 he took from the French, and rendered into pedestrian blank verse, a play called *Louis XI* which Irving later revived with great effect. In 1857 he adapted a French play, *Les Pauvres de Paris,* turned it into a blood-and-thunder melodrama designed for an American management, and called it *The Poor of New York.* In 1860 he made a stage adaptation of a novel, called it *The Colleen Bawn* and with it laid the foundation of a great reputation as an observer of the manners and customs of his native Ireland. In 1864 he re-wrote *The Poor of New York,* adapting it to the English scene and toning down the melodrama in deference to English taste, and had a run of 209 performances with it under the title of *The Streets of London.* There is no doubt at all that Boucicault was a very competent stage carpenter, but that he should have passed for a major dramatist is the cruellest possible comment on the English-speaking theatre of his day.

The fact was that the theatre was socially disreputable and artistically despised. Actors were still not received in good society. The undisputed leader of the English stage in the previous generation, William Charles Macready, a man of the highest culture and distinction, had retired in 1851 into the country, where his self-respect was constantly being affronted by the refusal of prejudiced neighbours to be neighbourly. No writer of real eminence would demean himself to write for the stage; or if any did, they adopted a lofty attitude and refused to learn the practical side of the dramatist's job. In consequence, dramatic writing had fallen into the hands of second-rate scribblers who were quite content that their work should be not only derivative but also extremely unnatural. The language of the stage was a bombastic jargon completely unlike that of real life, and the audiences, knowing nothing better, were quite content to have its so.

Into this queer, dim world Tom Robertson brought unexpected light. In the few years permitted to him before he died at 42, he made innovations in the writing and staging of plays which were the beginning of revolutionary changes. In his series of comedies, of which *Ours* (1866), *Caste* (1867) and *School* (1869) are best remembered, he used dialogue which, stilted though it sounds to us, seemed astonishingly colloquial to the mid-Victorians. Also, he was the first of the stage-directors in the modern sense. Before his time, a room on the stage bore no resemblance to a real room. Its doors and windows were painted on the backcloth, its chairs were ranged in rows; and if two actors had a confidential scene to play they carried their chairs down to the footlights for the purpose and put them tidily back when done with. Robertson insisted on practicable doors with handles to them, and natural movements. And, fortunately for himself and for the theatre, Gilbert was Robertson's friend.

It is quite possible that the two men worked together, for though Gilbert's first successful play, *The Princess*, went to another management, his second, *The Palace of Truth*, was staged in November, 1870, with Robertson's sister Madge (afterwards Mrs. Kendal and later a much-feared and deeply respected Grand Old Lady of the British stage as Dame Madge Kendal) in the lead. Three more of Gilbert's plays, *Pygmalion and Galatea* (1871), *The Wicked World* (1873) and *Broken Hearts* (1875) were staged by the Kendals after Tom Robertson's death, and it is clear that the connection was a close one. Gilbert, at any rate, had watched Robertson at work and admired his method of stage management. As a stage director, he was Robertson's disciple, if not his pupil.

As a dramatist, however, he was far from being Robertson's disciple, for his early work, so far from being realistic in tone, was mostly in blank verse. *The Princess* was described as a whimsical allegory and a " respectful perversion " of Tennyson's poem of the same name, about a beautiful princess who cut herself off from the world of men to found a women's university, and was naturally written in the same metre as its original. *The Palace of Truth*, a three-act fairy comedy on the idea of an enchanted palace in which everybody is magically compelled to speak the exact truth without knowing that he is doing so, was also written in blank verse; so were all the other three plays produced by the Kendals. As a prose-writer, Gilbert's chief achievements during these years were *Randall's Thumb* (1871), *Charity* (1874) and *Sweethearts* (1874), three poor plays whose stilted style made it clear that their author was not free of the outworn tradition of his time. One shining quality all these plays had, however. Excepting *The Princess*, an avowed parody, all of them were original. They came, not from the French, but from their author's imagination.

In 1875, therefore, at the age of 39, Gilbert was a man with two separate reputations. Outside the theatre he was known as a master of topsy-turvy humour of a kind entirely his own. Inside the theatre he was an assiduous dramatist who combined a neat trick of versification with a pleasant touch of fantasy, who had, however, hardly made the grade as yet in a big way. Still, he was established. And so one day an astute theatre-manager, Richard D'Oyle Carte, meeting Gilbert in the street, had the idea of inviting him to write a one-act piece to be set to music by Sullivan. Gilbert and Sullivan knew each other already, having met first in the autumn of 1870 and having collaborated in a two-act operetta called *Thespis, or The Gods Grown Old*, which had been staged in 1871 without much success. Gilbert happened to have something by him, and consented to let Carte read it. The result was *Trial By Jury*.

Gilbert, for some reason, had fallen out of love with his libretto by the time he read it to Sullivan, and did so with a growing air of disgust and indignation. Sullivan was delighted with it, however, and set it in a fortnight. It was staged as an after-piece to Offenbach's *La Perichole* at the Royalty Theatre on March 25th, 1875, made the success of the evening, and ran for 128 performances. This was enough to fix in D'Oyly Carte's mind the certainty that these two men were born to work in partnership, and from that time on the idea of providing them with a theatre to work in and a company to work for never left him. Putting that idea in practice was not a very easy matter, however. Gilbert still thought of himself as a serious dramatist in the making, while Sullivan, whose reputation as a serious musician was already made, was told on all hands that he must not on any account demean himself by working at light opera, of all things, and in the theatre, of all places.

For although the theatre was now beginning to rise from the social abyss, it was still almost entirely an actor's theatre. Henry Irving, who had finally established his position as uncrowned king of the British stage with his production of *Hamlet* at the Lyceum in 1874, was now beginning to occupy a position in London society such as no theatre man except Sheridan, and no actor except perhaps Garrick, had ever before been allowed to hold. What was more, he was doing something which neither Garrick nor Sheridan could have dreamed possible—he was forcing public opinion to accept not only himself as leader of the stage, but stage people in general as members of a reputable and respectable profession.

But Irving was an actor, and nothing but an actor. To him, the actor was the only artist of any consequence in the theatre, and such men as writers or musicians or scene-

31

designers existed only to give the actor his various appur-
tenances. Irving enjoyed a supreme position in the English
theatre for something like thirty years—thirty years which
saw the emergence of a whole new race of distinguished
dramatists, men like Pinero and Barrie and Shaw—yet in all
that time he never appeared in a new play by any of these
men, though Barrie wrote *The Professor's Love Story* and
Shaw *The Man of Destiny* specially for him. In those days
the Great Men of every art took themselves, and expected to
be taken, very seriously indeed; there could be no place for
writers or musicians of real eminence in a theatre whose
leader felt no need of them. And so in 1875 and for many
years after that, no really ambitious writer or musician could
work in the theatre, especially the frivolous-minded light-
operatic theatre, without some loss of self-respect.

Not for another two years, then, was D'Oyly Carte able
to get his team together again, and in that time Gilbert made
one more attempt to conquer the serious stage with a
portentous piece of fustian called *Dan'l Druce, Blacksmith*
(1876). This made no stir, and he followed it with a fairly
successful farce, *Engaged,* which perhaps reconciled him to
the idea of writing another libretto. At all events he did
yield to Carte's persuasions and wrote *The Sorcerer* in the
same year, 1877. Meanwhile Sullivan had been adding to his
serious fame in the concert-halls and had achieved enormous
popularity with his songs. But he was ready to set *The
Sorcerer,* and with that piece's production at the Opera
Comique Theatre on November 17th, 1877, the Gilbert and
Sullivan partnership made its real bow to the public.

Once the D'Oyly Carte Company had been formed, Gilbert
stepped confidently to its head as stage director. Now, at
last, he was able to apply the lessons he had learnt and the
principles he had evolved for himself when watching Tom
Robertson at work. Hitherto, when plays of his had been

W. S. Gilbert.

Arthur S. Sullivan.

" I am the monarch of the sea."
[Martyn Green as Sir Joseph Porter, K.C.B.,
in *H.M.S. Pinafore*]

produced, rehearsals had been one long battle between himself and temperamental star players who were not accustomed to being told what to do; and hitherto, to his fury, he had generally had to give way. Now that he had a say in choosing his company, therefore, he decided that it should contain no stars at all. Everybody would have to do exactly as he said, and if people objected, or tried to put on airs, he had a quick mind and a blistering tongue, and would put them without hesitation or mercy back in their places.

He was by nature a martinet, but he had also the quality which makes a martinet respected—an exact knowledge of what he wanted and how to get it. Very soon, stories began to be circulated about the ferocious discipline he exercised, but nearly all these anecdotes were told in a tone which admitted, ruefully, that he was right. There was one about an actress who objected to some piece of stage business— " I'm not a chorus-girl," she said, and got the answer, " No, madam, your voice isn't strong enough or you would be." There was one about an old actor who did a small gesture wrong again and again, and finally told Gilbert he was sick of being told he was wrong and had been on the stage long enough; " I agree," said Gilbert, and sacked him on the spot. Sometimes the retort was less abrupt, though the sequel was the same, as one lady found when she said she had always done so-and-so in Italian opera. " Unfortunately," said Gilbert, who was rehearsing *H.M.S. Pinafore* at the time, " this is not Italian opera, but only a burlesque of the lowest possible kind."

Against a man like this, it was impossible for anybody to prevail. He used to come to rehearsal with every stage move already clear in his mind, having worked them out with wooden blocks—one size for men, another, slightly smaller, for women—in a model theatre at home. He gave his actors every inflection and every gesture, and hot-tempered though he was and liable to unreasonable rages when opposed, he was endlessly patient and kind with those who tried to give him what he wanted. And so, in the very midst of a theatrical London in which the actors were having things all their own way, Gilbert established not merely the first but an outstandingly complete example of the modern " director's theatre," in which not individual acting but perfect teamwork is the chief aim.

Once the D'Oyly Carte Company was fully established, Gilbert gave up his attempts to get himself accepted as a serious dramatist. That he did so with some reluctance we may well believe, for it quite commonly happens that an artist undervalues the work that he does with ease, and is eager to be recognised for the work which costs him toil and anxiety. Gilbert himself once said that he had put more of himself into *Broken Hearts* than into any of his comic writings; but if anybody were to stage this blank-verse fairy play to-day it would be dismissed by any normal audience as a piece of intolerable sentimentality.

To-day it is quite painfully obvious that Gilbert lacked the first fundamental quality of the serious dramatist—the ability to create living characters. Not one of the people he invented has any inner life, or is seen in true proportion. All are distorted, the comic figures (rightly and properly) by Gilbertian satire, the serious ones by sheer staginess. As a comic writer, Gilbert was original both in matter and in manner; as a serious dramatist he was ahead of his time because he invented his stories instead of borrowing them, but he wrote them in the bombastic language of tradition. He was not unsuccessful in that style, for *Pygmalion and Galatea* was revived again and again and brought him a considerable fortune. But he had to admit in the end that his true bent was for fantastic comedy and satire, and as a practical man of the theatre he bowed to a decision forced upon him by his public.

34

But even in that domain, where he was undisputed master and made his own rules, his public vogue would have been short if he had stuck to the legitimate stage. The reason is simple. He liked writing about fairies, and fairies happened to be in fashion. It amused both Gilbert and his audiences, in that age of rigid respectability and immovable class distinctions, to imagine a race of beings who could set society at nought; and it amused Gilbert to identify these beings with the traditional characters of the Christmas pantomime. For instance, in *The Fairy's Dilemma,* produced as late as 1904, trouble arises because a fairy transforms a prim curate and a high-born young lady into Harlequin and Columbine, so that they have to go dancing about the streets to the constant outrage of their finer feelings.

To the Victorians, the spectacle of a duke's daughter, clad in the short skirts of the wicked ballet-stage, compelled to cavort in public and trying hard to keep her ducal dignity while so employed, would have been irresistibly (because rather shockingly) funny. But in 1904 Queen Victoria was in her grave, and the age to which she gave her name was definitely over. The new king, Edward VII, extended his friendship to people whose existence his mother would hardly have admitted, and respectability was becoming daily less rigid. If a duke's daughter wished to dress as a Columbine she could now do so openly at fancy-dress dances in the ballrooms of good society; and so the high-born lady in *The Fairy's Dilemma,* covered with shame at her short skirts, seemed in 1904 no longer shocking but out-of-date and rather silly. Besides, the actress who played her, Violet Vanbrugh, was herself the daughter not of a duke, it is true, but of a dignitary of the Church of England, which to Victorian ideas would have been almost as terrible. In a society bent on turning itself upside down there was no need of a supernatural agency to do it. The play failed.

Gilbert's vogue as a writer of straight comedy may be said, then, to have ended with Queen Victoria's death in 1901. If it had not been for the despised Gilbert and Sullivan compositions, he would have shared the fate of other leading dramatists of his own day—Pinero and Henry Arthur Jones in particular—of outliving his popularity and knowing himself unwanted by a new generation of audiences. As it was, he died a national figure, internationally mourned.

CHAPTER III

"*Trial by Jury*" *and* "*The Sorcerer*"

As we have seen, the first Gilbert and Sullivan composition made no great impression either upon its creators or upon the public. *Thespis, or the Gods Grown Old,* was presented at the Gaiety Theatre on December 23rd, 1871, by John Hollingshead, ran its course, and vanished unlamented.

On the face of it, this was a great chance missed. The Gaiety under Hollingshead was a theatre of great fame as the home of a peculiar form of Victorian light entertainment called burlesque. So strong is stage tradition that the idea persists even now among old playgoers that these shows were of a very high order of theatrical merit. A contemporary saying about "keeping the sacred lamp of burlesque burning" is constantly finding its way into print, and the names of some of the best-known comic writers of the time are connected with it. A little investigation shows that the truth came something short of this. So far as the writing was concerned, these burlesques were chiefly topical perversions of classical stories, written in doggerel verse which relied for its effect on a series of the most shameless puns that ingenious minds could fashion. As often happens when stage writing is of low quality, these strange concoctions were put across the footlights by a magnificent team of players, and the public asked nothing better for a time than to be given dose after dose of the same mixture. In *Thespis,* Gilbert was expected to conform to the regular Gaiety type of show, and it was no doubt because he had ideas and methods of his own that he failed to appeal to Hollingshead's specialised audience.

Thespis fell, in fact, between two schools. It did not

37

torture the English language enough for those to whom puns, and puns alone, were comic; and it had in it very little of Gilbert's own special brand of humour. The story, how a team of actors climbed Mount Olympus for a picnic, and changed places for a year with the tired old gods, was not given any special point or satirical twist. The piece vanished and was forgotten, except that one chorus, " Climbing over rocky mountain," was transferred later, with a few trifling verbal alterations, to *The Pirates of Penzance* and used for the entry of Major-General Stanley's daughters.

Neither Gilbert nor Sullivan made any effort to continue the collaboration; nobody in fact but D'Oyly Carte seems to have realised its possibilities, and even he took no action for three years. Once *Trial By Jury* had made its success, however, he knew that this was no ordinary partnership, and began to take steps at once to keep them together, writing full-length light operas for a permanent company. And once Carte's idea took practical shape, Gilbert's problem, how to get the best out of himself in the theatre, was solved whether he knew it or not.

Gilbert's great assets were three—his own special brand of topsy-turvy humour; his unrivalled faculty for immaculately-polished light verse; his superb sense of the theatre. If he allowed Carte to have his way, all these would be given full scope; and in addition, he would be able to indulge his liking for stories with a strong element of magic or fantasy, for the musical stage is by its very nature a fantastic place where miracles and absurdities are part of normal experience. The best proof that Gilbert as a librettist was in his own element is the fact that nearly all his early libretti were based on writings of his own already in print. *Trial By Jury*, for example, was simply a recasting in dramatic form of something he had already had published in the pages of *Fun*.

As a result, it was completely characteristic. Its subject was characteristic, for Gilbert's superlatively logical mind was always fascinated by the law. He was a lawyer by profession, for having made a thoroughly unhappy start in life in a Government office, he inherited £400 from an aunt, used the money to qualify as a barrister, and practised without notable success for four years before his journalistic work began to bring him enough money to live on. Its manner was characteristic also, for it was just like Gilbert to take a dull, dry, sordid affair like a breach of promise trial and, with a miraculous blend of legal fact and operatic fancy, make it supremely funny. As a lawyer, he knew well enough that in real life these cases often come unpleasantly near to a form of legalised blackmail, and that while the man who jilts a woman is no credit to his sex, the woman who is ready to put a price on her broken heart is hardly an ornament to hers. Gilbert contrived both to lay satirical emphasis on, and to remove, the unpleasantness by plunging the whole affair into a bath of high-flowing operatic emotion.

From these emotions not one of the characters is free, from the learned Judge on the bench to the least-regarded juryman in the box. The Defendant when he enters is greeted with howls of execration and threats of damages by the jurors. The lovely Plaintiff, arriving accompanied by a chorus of bridesmaids wearing garlands of roses, makes instant capture of the hearts not only of her own counsel, but of judge and jury as well, and she sobs on the breasts of each of them in turn. The climax comes when the Judge, tiring suddenly of the proceedings, brings them to an end by announcing that he is going to marry the lady himself.

Short as it is, and written in cantata form with no spoken dialogue, *Trial By Jury* is of very great importance in any study of the Gilbert and Sullivan operas, because in it we can see Gilbert's work as a librettist beginning to take shape.

Much of the pattern on which the full-length operas were to
be designed has still to be hammered out, but a surprising
amount of it is there already. Consider, for instance, the
Judge's song. Not only is it the first of a whole series of
autobiographical songs, in each of which a Very Important
Person explains how he came to be so very important; it is
one of the best and most famous of that series. Like the
Major-General in *The Pirates of Penzance,* like Sir Joseph
Porter in *H.M.S. Pinafore,* the Judge blandly gives away the
fact that his right to hold his eminent position is doubtful, to
say the least of it:

> In Westminster Hall I danced a dance
>> Like a semi-despondent fury;
> For I thought I should never hit on a chance
>> Of addressing a British jury—
> But I soon got tired of third-class journeys
>> And dinners of bread and water;
> So I fell in love with a rich attorney's
>> Elderly, ugly daughter.

The rich attorney makes the young man's fortune for him,
and then:

> At length I became as rich as the Gurneys
>> An incubus then I thought her,
> So I thew over that rich attorney's
>> Elderly, ugly daughter.
> The rich attorney my character high
>> Tried vainly to disparage—
> And now, if you please, I'm ready to try
>> This breach of promise of marriage.

This is the true Gilbert, the sardonic humorist with the
individual mind which had made his fame as a writer, coming
into his own on the stage at last. And a little later comes
a duet for Plaintiff and Defendant which also shows that

underneath his gay nonsense he has an eye for human
weaknesses, and has not lost sight of the fact that the chief
object of anybody who sues for breach of promise is to get
money. The Plaintiff flings herself into the Defendant's
arms, and sings:

> I love him—I love him—with fervour unceasing
>   I worship and madly adore;
> My blind adoration is always increasing,
>   My loss I shall ever deplore.
> Oh, see what a blessing—what love and caressing
>   I've lost, and remember it, pray,
> When you I'm addressing are busy assessing
>   The damages Edwin must pay.

The Defendant, seeing his bank-balance in danger, repels
her roughly and begins to cry down his value in this market:

> I smoke like a furnace—I'm always in liquor,
>   A ruffian—a bully—a sot;
> I'm sure I should thrash her—perhaps I should kick her,
>   I am such a very bad lot!
> I'm not prepossessing, as you may be guessing,
>   She couldn't endure me a day;
> Recall my professing when you are assessing
>   The damages Edwin must pay!

The law and its processes do not change much as the years
go by. Breach of promise suits (perhaps because women
occupy a different economic position) do not happen now as
often as in 1876, but they do happen. Technical legal terms
are the same now as they were then, and there is little in
Trial By Jury which does not explain itself to a modern
audience. It may, however, be worth while to call the
reader's attention to the end of the chorus in which the Jury-
men express their lack of sympathy with the Defendant:

> He shall treat us with awe
> If there isn't a flaw
> Singing so merrily—trial-la-law!

" Trial-la-law " is a particularly atrocious pun on " tra-la-la," and it shows that although Gilbert was beginning to go his own way to work, he had not yet entirely shaken of the influence of the burlesque tradition.

The originality of *Trial By Jury*, and the fact that the public liked it better than Offenbach's *La Perichole*, which it was intended to supplement, convinced D'Oyly Carte that his librettist and composer were made for one another, little though they seemed to think so themselves. He demanded a full-length book from Gilbert, and set about finding a theatre and financial backers. But Gilbert, as we have already seen, was in no hurry; not for another two years would he accept defeat as a serious dramatist. Then, early in 1877, once more using one of his own stories as his source, he wrote *The Sorcerer*. Even now, there was a further delay. Sullivan's brother Fred, who had played the Judge in *Trial by Jury* and for whom the name-part in *The Sorcerer* was intended, had just died, and Sullivan was too sunk in grief to be able to write light music for the moment. Later in the year he finished the task, and on November 17th, at the Opera Comique, the D'Oyly Carte Company came into being.

The Sorcerer ran for 175 performances—not a success on the scale to which the partnership became accustomed later, but a success nevertheless. To-day, the D'Oyly Carte Company sometimes includes it in the repertoire but more commonly leaves it out. It has some excellent songs, and the Sorcerer's own song, " My name is John Wellington Wells," has its own individual fame. But the plot is unsatisfactory, the ending lacks Gilbert's customary ingenuity, and there is an air of tentativeness, due of course to inexperience in this particular form, about the whole piece. However, it provided a good start for Carte's project, and enabled Gilbert to collect the kind of company he wanted and to impose the kind of discipline he believed in. It is significant that he engaged for two of the chief male parts two quite unknown actors, George Grossmith and Rutland Barrington, who became twin mainstays of the company and created all the chief Gilbertian comic parts between them. Grossmith was in fact not an actor at all, but a drawing-room and concert entertainer who was mortally afraid of losing his dates with the Young Men's Christian Association if he went on the stage.

Theatrically and socially, *The Sorcerer* is a period piece. Much of its dialogue is written in blank verse, which is intended to be set to music as recitative and naturally employs high-sounding language; but even when it drops into prose the drop is not of noticeable depth. Here, for example, is Dr. Daly, Vicar of Ploverleigh, soliloquising after an interview with one of the village girls who is in love with him but dares not say so:

> Poor little girl! I'm afraid she has something on her mind. She is rather comely. Time was when this old heart would have throbbed in double time at the sight of such a fairy form! But tush! I am puling! Here comes the young Alexis, with his proud and happy father. Let me dry this tell-tale tear!

To us, this is pure parody of a by-gone stage idiom, and no doubt when Gilbert wrote " But tush! I am puling!" he was going for the laugh. But the disconcerting fact is that the language in which Gilbert wrote his serious plays is so like the passage just quoted that we can hardly tell when he was deliberately exaggerating the style in order to be laughed

43

at and when he was expecting to be taken with deadly seriousness. That is one reason why his libretti have lasted so much better that his plays. The plays can no longer be taken seriously, but the libretti can still be laughed at. All the same, it is worth noting as we pass that the three operas in which the dialogue is written either in verse or in highly artificial prose—*The Sorcerer, Princess Ida* and *Ruddigore*— are much less certain of their places in the repertoire to-day than the others, in which the dialogue is nearer the everyday English of Gilbert's own time.

The setting of *The Sorcerer,* in the opening act, is the garden of a large Elizabethan country house—the kind of stately home which every successful Englishman of 1877 had an ambition to own. The country-house era continued until 1914 in its full glory, but after the first World War all the great houses and many of the moderate-sized ones became a problem and a burden to their owners, while now, after the second World War, such places can only be maintained and staffed by a few people so fabulously rich that they can go on living indefinitely on capital. Most of these mansions have ceased to be private houses; they are hotels, clubs, hospitals or official headquarters.

In 1877, however, it was accepted as an immutable law that the barriers of class were almost impregnable. A hymn very popular at the time said so in plain terms:

> The rich man in his castle
> The poor man at his gate,
> God made them, high and lowly,
> And ordered their estate.

Gilbert believed firmly in class distinctions, and though he sometimes laughed at snobs and was always ready to attack pretentiousness of any kind, he did feel that the greatest happiness for the greatest number was achieved when people were content to stick to their stations. On that feeling,

44

the plot of *The Sorcerer* is based. The villagers of Plover-leigh have come to Sir Marmaduke Pointdextre's garden to celebrate the betrothal of Sir Marmaduke's son Alexis to Aline, daughter of Lady Sangazure, whose family is so old that it goes back in direct descent to Helen of Troy. Everybody is delighted at the prospect of so suitable a match, and the villagers are delighted at the prospect of the large and lavish tea which Sir Marmaduke is providing to mark the occasion.

Everybody is satisfied, in fact, except Alexis himself. Alexis has ideas. He is a self-appointed missionary in the cause of love and marriage, and holds the belief that love can, and should, level all ranks. He has been lecturing at mechanics' institutes on the idea that working men ought to marry countesses, and complains that while the working men seem all in favour of the scheme, the countesses hang back. Happy in his own love for his Aline, he wants to be sure on his betrothal day that all the people on his estate shall be equally happy, and so he has engaged a sorcerer from London to come to the party and doctor the tea with a love-philtre, the effect of which will be to produce violent love at first sight between any two people of opposite sexes who have both drunk the brew.

This is a far-fetched and complicated idea, very different from the simple and logical inversions on which the more famous operas are based, and we can only imagine that a good deal of what Gilbert considered sentimental twaddle must have been talked at the time about love as a leveller, for otherwise he could not have expected his public to laugh at Alexis and his theories. Here is the young man, rhapsodising to Aline:

> Oh that the world would break down the artificial
> barriers of rank, wealth, education, age, beauty,

> habits, taste and temper, and recognise the glorious
> principle that in marriage alone is to be found the
> panacea for every ill!

Unless there were people about who were in the habit of
talking recognisably like that, the satire could have had no
bite. It was a safe and secure age, in which all sorts of
crazy doctrines were solemnly preached by people who knew
they never could be adopted.

Once launched on his plot, Gilbert was able to develop
several of his characteristic comic situations. In the first
act, much of the comedy centres on the unexpected traits of
John Wellington Wells, the sorcerer. It was always Gilbert's
way to treat the supernatural as something quite ordinary and
matter-of-fact. " Have you," says Alexis to Aline, " ever
heard of the firm of J. W. Wells and Co., the old-established
family sorcerers, in St. Mary Axe?" " I have seen their
advertisement," Aline answers, and establishes in the mind
of the audience the fact that Mr. Wells, magician though he
is, is just a City shopkeeper. When Mr. Wells is sent for,
Aline is frightened, and says very sensibly that Alexis cannot
protect her from a man who could turn her into a guinea-pig.
Alexis calms her fears:

> He *could* change you into a guinea-pig, no doubt,
> but it is most unlikely he would take any such
> liberty. It's a most respectable firm, and I am sure
> he would never be guilty of so untradesmanlike an
> act.

After that the appearance of Mr. Wells himself, a paragon
of middle-class respectability, who recommends his wares in
the language of any trade circular, brings the joke to its
climax and prepares the way for the song—the first of the
famous Gilbert and Sullivan patter-songs which carried

"Trial by Jury" and *"The Sorcerer"*

George Grossmith to fame and Henry Lytton, his chief
successor, to a knighthood:

> Oh! my name is John Wellington Wells
> I'm a dealer in magic and spells
>> In blessings and curses,
>> And ever-filled purses,
> In prophecies, witches and knells.
> If any one anything lacks
> He'll find it all ready in stacks
>> If he'll only look in
>> On the resident Djinn
> Number seventy, Simmery Axe.

> We've a first-rate assortment of magic;
>> And for raising a posthumous shade
> With effects that are comic or tragic
>> There's no cheaper house in the trade.
> Love-philtre—we've quantities of it;
>> And for knowledge if anyone burns
> We keep an extremely small prophet
>> Who brings us unbounded returns . . .

" Why a *small* prophet?" somebody may well ask at this
point. The answer is, to gratify, once again, the Victorian
passion for puns. There was a business slogan of those days—
" small profits, quick returns."

And so the first act of *The Sorcerer* rises to a mock-heroic
climax, first with the tremendous incantation with which
Mr. Wells summons the spirits to assist with the mixing of the
love-philtre and the pouring of the potion into the tea-pot,
and then with the entry of the villagers, whose chorus is a
parody on all the operatic rhapsodies ever written about the
pleasures of the table:—

47

Now to the banquet we press
　Now for the eggs, the ham,
Now for the mustard and cress,
　Now for the strawberry jam.
Now for the tea of our host,
　Now for the rollicking bun,
Now for the muffin and toast,
　Now for the gay Sally Lunn.

In the second act, the love-philtre is taking effect, with results which anybody less foolish than Alexis might have foreseen. He does not object when the villagers fall in love and beseech the Vicar, Dr. Daly, to marry them to the most unsuitable mates; that is all part of his scheme. He is not so pleased, however, when his father, Sir Marmaduke, falls in love, not suitably with Lady Sangazure, but most unsuitably with a respectable village woman, Dame Partlet. He is still less pleased when his own betrothed, Aline, whom he has forced to drink the philtre against her will, falls in love with the aged Dr. Daly. His views on love-philtres change suddenly, and he asks the sorcerer what is to be done. Mr. Wells says that the spell will be removed if either he himself or Alexis will consent to die, and after some characteristically Gilbertian argument which it is to be, Mr. Wells agrees to sacrifice himself. He vanishes, and all the other characters, properly paired off, accept Sir Marmaduke's invitation to another feast, and break into a general dance.

As will be seen from the foregoing account, the plot of *The Sorcerer* is one of Gilbert's least ingenious inventions, and its end is perfunctory in the extreme. On its own merits it could hardly have survived; but it has many charming and amusing incidental touches, and always commands interest among Gilbert and Sullivan devotees. And it paved the way for a much more workmanlike piece, which was in Sullivan's hands just before the end of 1877. " I have very little doubt whatever but you will be pleased with it," said Gilbert; and Sullivan showed his pleasure by getting to work on it at once, and completing it quickly in spite of continual and painful bouts of illness. It was *H.M.S. Pinafore*.

CHAPTER IV

" H.M.S. Pinafore "

In *H.M.S. Pinafore* Gilbert found the shape he had been fumbling after in *The Sorcerer* and from which he never afterwards departed in any marked degree. Now that he had got his company together, he could write parts designed to fit particular players. But the great innovation which he introduced with this opera, and which was thenceforward a constant asset, was a chorus which was not merely a band of singers who came on whenever wanted in dresses appropriate to the scene, but formed collectively an important character in the play.

Thespis and *Trial By Jury* had had choruses of no particular description, while the chorus of *The Sorcerer* consisted of villagers of different sorts, sizes and ages. They had no uniformity, and no function but to sing. In *H.M.S. Pinafore,* however, the men were the crew of the warship and opened the opera by introducing themselves as such:

> We sail the ocean blue
> And our saucy ship's a beauty,
> We're sober men and true
> And attentive to our duty . . .

The women's chorus were the sisters, cousins and aunts of Sir Joseph Porter. Their entry was heralded by the ship's captain:

> But see, Sir Joseph's barge approaches . . .
> accompanied by the admiring crowd of female
> relatives that attend him wherever he goes.

They, like the crew, remain themselves throughout, and, when occasion serves, take part in the action.

"H.M.S. Pinafore"

The alternative title of *H.M.S. Pinafore* is *The Lass That Loved a Sailor,* and as the lass in question is the Captain's daughter and the sailor is a member of the crew, the theme of the opera is really very much that of *The Sorcerer* over again, that love can level ranks. But the second plot Gilbert evolved from that theme was infinitely better than the first one. Once again he went to his own published works for material, and this time he laid his *Bab Ballads* (so called because he had used the signature " Bab " for them when they appeared in periodicals) freely under contribution. A poem called " Joe Golighty," about a sailor who wanted to marry the daughter of the First Lord of the Admiralty, gave him his main thread, but most of the ballads which deal with the Navy, and several which do not, gave him ideas for incidents or characters.

Gilbert loved the sea, and one of the first uses he made of the wealth that his writings brought him was to buy a yacht. His knowledge of the Navy was as exact as his knowledge of the law; and just as it pleased him to turn the law inside out in *Trial By Jury,* so it pleased him in *H.M.S. Pinafore* to turn the Navy inside out, by pretending that it was run on the lines of a girls' school. Captain Corcoran of the *Pinafore,* who says good morning to his crew in polite verse, never uses a big big D., and is hardly ever sick at sea, had had an obvious forerunner in *The Bab Ballads* in Captain Reece, who looked after his men so well on board the *Mantelpiece.* And the idea that the Navy would be shocked if it heard a swear-word had been anticipated in the ballad called " The Bishop of Rum-ti-Foo Again " :—

> Some sailors whom he did not know
> Had landed there not long ago
> And taught them " Bother!" also " Blow!"
>   (Of wickedness the germs.)
> No need to use a casuist's pen

> To prove that they were merchantmen;
> No sailor of the Royal N.
> Would use such awful terms.

The idea of babies being changed at birth and changing back when all was discovered is to be found in the Ballads, while " The Bumboat Woman's Story " anticipates Little Buttercup even to the detail of the peppermint drops she sells to the crew.

It was in *Pinafore,* too, that Gilbert began to work topical allusions into his songs, and in *Pinafore* that he made one of his very few excursions into political satire. He was no politician. He felt, as any successful man of those days might well feel, that things were pretty comfortable as they were; and as both the chief Parliamentary parties were of much the same opinion he had no interest in either of them. But he had the seaman's scorn of the " land-lubber," and when the Prime Minister chose W. H. Smith, the senior partner in the publishing and news-agency business which still bears his name, to be First Lord of the Admiralty, Gilbert's sense of the ridiculous sprang to life. He wrote a song for his own First Lord, Sir Joseph Porter, rather like the Judge's song in *Trial By Jury,* in which Sir Joseph explains the steps by which he rose to be " the Ruler of the Queen's Navee." He traces his career; from an attorney's office-boy polishing up the handle of the big front door he becomes junior clerk, articled clerk, partner, member of Parliament. And he ends with this advice:

> Now, landsmen all, whoever you may be,
> If you want to rise to the top of the tree,
> If your soul isn't fettered to an office stool,
> Be careful to be guided by this golden rule—
>   Stick close to your desk and never go to sea
>   And you all may be Rulers of the Queen's Navee.

Gilbert was so politically innocent that he thought nobody would suspect that in Sir Joseph Porter he was referring to Smith, because the two men's political views were different; but Smith has been " Pinafore Smith " in men's minds ever since.

H.M.S. Pinafore became the rage, both in London and in New York. It was produced at the Opera Comique in London on May 25th, 1878, and had the phenomenal run for those days of 700 performances. The New York run, which began in the following year, lasted for 178 performances—a success indeed, but on a distinctly smaller scale. Since in the two theatrical capitals Sullivan's music, Gilbert's book, and the novelty and fidelity of the setting (Gilbert had seen to it that every detail of the *Pinafore's* rigging was correct) had been received with equal rapture, the disparity in the two runs needs some explanation. The fact was that before the actual official version of the opera was produced *Pinafore* had been widely pirated; and the only reason why the official version ran as well as it did was that the pirates had not been able to reproduce Sullivan's orchestration.

Apart from that, however, it was not to be expected that all Gilbert's strokes of satire could be appreciated fully in New York, except by those playgoers who happened to know England and its rather confusing social system.

England is always a difficult country to understand from outside, because she manages at one and the same time to be nominally an aristocracy and a democracy in fact. Her citizens belong to rigidly divided social grades, and yet in practice can ignore class barriers and achieve a man-to-man equality not to be outdone anywhere. The class barriers were much more rigid in Gilbert's time than they are to-day. The country was peaceful and immensely prosperous, and the social hierarchy seemed to be a permanent institution in which all had their appointed positions. In those days " He knows his place " was a very high tribute to anybody, high or low; and " He doesn't know his place " was deep condemnation. Even the King had to know his place, and to realise that the real power of government lay not with the hereditary monarch but with an elected House of Commons. Three kings in our history have lost their thrones because they wanted to do something which the Commons would not stand for; and one of them, who tried to stand for his " rights," lost his head as well.

The sense of man-to-man equality might be seen operating everywhere. Watch a great Victorian landowner, a duke perhaps, giving orders to his game-keeper. Both men are easy, relaxed, familiar, because they are discussing a subject on which they have interests in common. There is no condescension on one side, no obsequiousness on the other, because each man knows his place and respects himself. And if next day the positions are reversed—if, for example, the Duke turns out to play cricket for the village team of which the game-keeper is captain—there is the same easy attitude. Here also each man knows his place. Unless he is himself a good cricketer, the Duke will not presume to interfere with his captain's handling of the game; and in any case he will not give advice unless it is asked for.

What makes England a puzzling place for the visitor to understand is that this free and equal intercourse exists, and is perfectly understood on both sides to exist, only while the two men are pursuing their common interest. It does not imply, as in some other countries it would be expected to imply, any relaxation of social barriers.

The English, in fact, have two codes of values always in operation—a normal code, in which all that matters is that a man should be a man, and a social code in which it is important that he should be a gentleman. It is difficult for other nations, and particularly for Americans, whose method of grading people is different, to grasp that this kind of class-consciousness is so ingrained in the English way of life that it is devoid of snobbery, and is offensive only to snobs. I once heard an American lady ask an Englishman what social standing a doctor would have in England, and I remember how startled she was to be told that his profession had little or no bearing on his social standing. And I myself once spent most of a long train-journey trying to soothe the shocked feelings of another American lady on discovering that the Principal and Vice-Principal of a certain women's college in England, though they were on excellent terms while on duty, did not visit one another's homes or have any private social intercourse at all. I told her that since the position was tacitly accepted on both sides it could give no hurt to anybody but a social climber; and I told her that I found equally shocking her assumption that because jars of oil and water happened to be kept on the same shelf they must be forced to mix. In the end, I persuaded her to agree, with some reluctance, that the English system must be all right for England, since it worked. But she still could not see what made it work.

In the England of to-day, where privilege has so largely been abolished, it is no longer of the first importance whether a man is, technically, a gentleman; but when *Pinafore* was written it mattered enormously. In the upper class of Victorian society birth counted for a great deal, breeding and manners for a great deal, money for very little. If you " belonged " you were accepted. If you could behave as if you belonged, you were accepted after scrutiny. If you could not behave, if you were a social climber, or in any way pretentious you were labelled cad or bounder, and frozen out, no matter how powerful or important you might be in another world. That was the theory, at any rate.

All this code of social values, Gilbert and his London

audiences knew perfectly. Consequently, when he proceeded in *Pinafore* to turn the whole code upside down and then to behave as if it were right way up, the result was a whole series of characteristic inversions which only an English audience, and indeed only an English audience of the mid-Victorian era, could appreciate to the full.

To show how completely he had turned the social relationships between his characters wrong way up, let me show you the four chief people of the opera—Captain Corcoran, his daughter Josephine, Sir Joseph Porter and Ralph Rackstraw as they would have been in real life.

First, Captain Corcoran. A Captain in the Navy is, by definition, " an officer and a gentleman " and has a prescriptive right to be accepted as such in the highest social circles. What is more, in Captain Corcoran's day officers in the Navy were almost invariably " gentlemen " by birth. The Navy, for reasons which I will explain lower down, was always a less democratic service than the Army, and promotion from the ranks, which was comparatively common on land, was almost unknown at sea. The Navy drew its officers very largely from a number of upper-class families which had the sea in their blood, and whose sons offered themselves to the Admiralty, generation after generation, as a matter of course. Furthermore, in Captain Corcoran's individual case, we have Little Buttercup's direct evidence:

> Two tender babes I nussed:
> One was of low condition,
> The other, upper crust,
> A regular patrician.

Captain Corcoran has always had reason to believe that he is this " high-born babe."

On board the Pinafore he occupies one of the most autocratic positions a Briton can hold. It is old Navy custom that the captain of a warship lives alone, segregated even from the rest of the officers, in quarters whose spaciousness is palatial compared to theirs. His word is law, and nobody else —not even an admiral who has chosen the vessel as his flagship—can give the Pinafore direct orders. He has been brought up from the age of 12 or so in the tradition of absolute discipline, he knows his place exactly, and on board will stand no nonsense from anybody, no matter how mild may be his temper on shore.

His daughter Josephine is therefore in real life very much what she seems to Ralph Rackstraw in the opera—a Victorian young lady of high birth, very sure of her social position, and hardly conscious of the existence of her father's crew as individuals. In her time the class-barrier between an officer's lady and an able seaman was absolute—so absolute that the passage of 70 years has not yet completely broken it down. In 1949 a comedy was produced in London, written by a naval officer and his wife, in which the main situation was the scandal caused in naval circles because an officer's sister, a schoolmistress by profession, gave a few private lessons in the King's English to a sailor who was anxious to qualify for a commission. This seemed absurd snobbery to the critics and the public in London, and the play failed there; but at Portsmouth, in naval circles at any rate, it was accepted as a piece of simple realism. It will therefore be understood that in 1878 the idea that Josephine could not merely be aware of Ralph's existence, but actually fall in love with him, was something so far-fetched as to be thinkable only in comic opera, and fantastic Gilbertian comic opera at that.

Partly the reason for this is that Ralph himself, in real life, would be hardly fit company for a lady. I said above that the Navy had always been a less democratic service than the Army, and now we come to the reason for this. The Army was a volunteer service, the Navy had to use compulsion.

War on land, in those days when war was a picturesque adventure, almost a sport, attracted a constant supply of spirited young men to the colours. War by sea, in sailing-ships which were small, slow and unhealthy, with bad food and no comfort, attracted only a few. Recruiting for Nelson's Navy was done by press-gangs which found it less troublesome to look for their men among the roughest types. To deal with such men, a brutal age prescribed brutal discipline, and the tradition of toughness had by no means died out in the Navy of Gilbert's time. There are casual references all over the Bab Ballads to show that Gilbert took the cat-o'-nine-tails, the rope's end and the black-hole as necessary, if regrettable, adjuncts to life at sea. And so while a lady like Josephine might quite possibly find a romantic young soldier to fall in love with, romantic young sailors, who could speak to her in a language she could understand, were practically non-existent.

Finally, Sir Joseph Porter. Alone among the characters, he lacks—in real life—that Victorian virtue of knowing his place, because his place, officially and socially, is moving rapidly upwards. Too rapidly, in fact. To Victorian ideas, the industrious office-boy who rose to be a junior clerk, an articled clerk and a partner in an attorney's firm was an entirely admirable figure. None of these jobs was the kind of job that a gentleman would do (for if a gentleman took to the law in those days he became a barrister, not a solicitor); but the man who did them well was an able fellow and a good citizen, to whom people like Captain Corcoran and his daughter were civil, so long as they were not expected to treat him as an equal, or to invite him to their home except on business. But the final stage in Sir Joseph's progress makes him a social problem:

"H.M.S. Pinafore"

I grew so rich that I was sent
By a pocket borough* into Parliament.
I always voted at my party's call
And I never thought of thinking for myself at all.
   I thought so little, they rewarded me
   By making me the Ruler of the Queen's Navee.

Now, what are the Corcorans to do? Officially, Sir Joseph
has become a Cabinet Minister, an important personage, and
when he comes on board H.M.S. Pinafore he must be
received with every outward sign of courtesy and respect.
Socially, however, he is no more a gentleman now than he
was before his appointment to his high office, and unless he
shows by his behaviour that he knows his place in his new
position he will not be accepted. Josephine and her father
will regard him as " that little jumped-up lawyer," and if
he throws his weight about or offends against the code of
good manners proper to the occasion, he will be made to feel
that under their show of respect these people despise him.

I hope it now begins to be clear with what a network of
absurdities Gilbert presented the delighted London public of
1878 in the plot of *H.M.S. Pinafore*. To begin with, of
course, there is the vocabulary in which Ralph Rackstraw,
the common and uneducated sailor, " the meanest tar that
ploughs the water," expresses himself. Listen to him,
explaining himself to Josephine:

> In me there meet a combination of antithetical
> elements which are at eternal war with one another.
> Driven hither by objective influences—thither by
> subjective emotions—wafted one moment into
> blazing day by mocking hope—plunging the next
> into the Cimmerian darkness of tangible despair, I

---

* Pocket boroughs, which were actually abolished in 1832, were
boroughs which had the right to return members to Parliament,
but in which there were no voters. What Gilbert means is that
Sir Joseph was not elected to Parliament, but bought his way in.

am but a living ganglion of irreconcilable antagonisms. I hope I make myself clear, lady?

" Perfectly," says Josephine; and then, to point the incongruity, she adds, to herself (and the audience), " His simple eloquence goes to my heart."

Then there is Captain Corcoran's arrival, and the highly unusual polite greetings between him and his crew, followed by the song in which he proudly claims, " Though ' bother it ' I may occasionally say, I never use a big, big D."

But the crowning pitch of topsy-turvydom is reached when Sir Joseph Porter comes aboard. The absurd deference with which he is received, the absurd airs he puts on, the ridiculous way in which he interferes with arrangements, the liberties he takes with the ship's discipline, and finally his calm assumption that because he is a Cabinet Minister he is *socially* far above Captain Corcoran and Josephine—all these add to the effect of wild caricature, so that for those who are familiar with the real set-out there is hardly a word Sir Joseph speaks or a gesture he makes which does not carry a laugh.

Josephine is allowed once, and once only, to put into words the real effect upon her of Sir Joseph's behaviour:

It is useless—Sir Joseph's attentions nauseate me. I know he is a truly great and good man, but to me he seems tedious, fretful and dictatorial.

Then she goes back to Gilbertian exaggeration:

Yet his must be a mind of no common order, or he would not dare to teach my dear father to dance a hornpipe on the cabin table.

Absurd as such an idea is, it is hardly further away from likelihood than Sir Joseph's remarks about " a humble captain's child " a little later on, when he sings to Josephine:

Never mind the why and wherefore,
  Love can level ranks, and therefore
Though your nautical relation
  In my set could scarcely pass—
Though you occupy a station
  In the lower middle class—
Ring the merry bells on board ship,
  Rend the air with warbling wild
For the union of my lordship
  With a humble captain's child.

This stands the whole social fabric neatly upside down, for those who realise that it is Sir Joseph himself who comes from " the lower middle class," and that no officer in the Navy of that day could ever have belonged to it at all.

I have gone into this class question at some length, because it establishes once and for all in the minds of readers the kind of society in which Gilbert lived, and with which on the whole he was very well content. Gilbert's was a very common-sensible mind, and his chief objection to idealistic schemes was simply his belief that they would not work. In *The Sorcerer* and *H.M.S. Pinafore* his theme was the absurdity of the idea that love levels all ranks, and he therefore deals in those two operas with the social scene more directly than in any of his subsequent works except the little-known *Utopia Limited*.

For my special purpose it was necessary to give a general sketch of that particular corner of civilisation which Gilbert knew; and the fact that I have been able to do so early in this book will save a good deal of tedious explanation later on.

CHAPTER V

" The Pirates of Penzance "

Least of all the early Gilbert and Sullivan operas does *The Pirates of Penzance* owe its origin to Gilbert's previous writings. It depends on the fusion of two very characteristic ideas—that a man may be so completely at the mercy of his sense of duty as to obey it no matter what the cost, and that the 21st birthday of a person born in Leap Year on the 29th February does not occur until that person is at least 84 years old.

The first of these two ideas, which is embodied in the opera's alternative title, *The Slave of Duty,* had indeed been glanced at already in the Bab Ballads. At duty's call the obedient family of Captain Reece had broken off their engagements to members of the aristocracy and had become the wives of the crew of *The Mantelpiece.* The Leap Year idea had been used by Gilbert before in an entertainment written in his early days, and once he had decided to use it again the plot of *The Pirates* followed logically, almost inevitably. In order that the situation of the Slave of Duty should be as desperate as possible, obviously he must have been apprenticed to a profession which he loathed. How could this most effectively be brought about? Obviously, by mistake. And so the preposterous notion of the deaf nursery-maid who thought her master said " pirate " when he had in fact said " pilot " comes into Gilbert's mind, and a worthy successor to *Pinafore* is assured.

The Pirates is unique in one respect. It is the only one of the operas to have been originally produced in New York. This was done to establish copyright, and Sullivan carried out much of his share of the collaboration actually in America.

"*The Pirates of Penzance*"

It was produced on December 31st, 1879, amid stringent precautions to avoid the risk that *The Pirates* would be pirated; and it did not open at the Opera Comique in London till April 3rd, 1880—though a scratch performance, necessary to establish copywright, had been given before the New York opening.

In several ways, there is an affinity between this opera and *Pinafore*. In both pieces there is a men's chorus consisting of a ship's crew; and though the Pinafore's men are afloat and the Pirate King's crew are ashore, a nautical flavour is common to both. In both pieces, also, the ladies' chorus consists of female relations of the character played by George Grossmith. Gilbert even goes so far as to allow Major-General Stanley to emphasise this affinity by a direct reference:

> " Then I can hum a fugue, of which I've heard
> the music's din afore,
> And whistle all the airs from that infernal
> nonsense, *Pinafore*."

With *The Pirates* it became clear that the partners could repeat not simply the form but much of the success of *Pinafore*. The new piece quickly settled down to a run of 383 performances—not equal to that of its predecessor, but good enough.

So far I have laid stress chiefly on the similarities between the two pieces, but now it is time to point out one fundamental dissimilarity. Most of my last chapter was spent in explaining the many points of contact which Gilbert's travesty in *Pinafore* had with the real life of mid-Victorian England. In *The Pirates of Penzance* there were almost no such points of contact at all. The place where the events take place is described as " A rocky sea-shore on the coast of Cornwall," but it bears no such relationship to the real Cornwall as the setting of *H.M.S. Pinafore* does to the real Portsmouth. It is a purely imaginary Cornwall, in which pirates belonging to an earlier century and a wilder civilisation come to grips with policemen of 1880. In such a Cornwall, anything at all may happen, and is no more expected to make sense than the title of the opera makes sense. For why are these pirates described as " of Penzance," when they never go near that respectable little seaside town, and would be arrested at once if they did?

We are, then, in a world of fantasy; and this is made crystal clear in the first few moments of the opera's action. Frederic, the hero, the slave of duty, has reached the age of 21, and as the curtain rises the pirates are celebrating the fact that he has served his apprenticeship, is out of his indentures, and is now entitled to call himself a full-blown member of the band. At once we are presented with the surprising spectacle of a group of outlawed cut-throats run on the lines of a respectable calling. An even more startling picture follows almost immediately, for when Frederic announces that the first use he is going to make of his freedom is to leave the band for ever, the Pirate King's remark is:

> But this is quite unaccountable; a keener hand at
> scuttling a Cunarder or cutting out a White Star
> never shipped a hand spike.

No doubt the vessels of the Cunard or White Star lines of 1880 would seem unimpressively small compared with the enormous floating hotels of the present day, but compared with the Pirate King's schooner, which in Gilbert's original stage-direction was to be seen at anchor on the backcloth, they were both large and fast. The notion that Frederic had had experience of overhauling and boarding any of them could only exist in the topsy-turvy world of Gilbert's fancy. And so the story goes on, being solemnly reasonable about wildly unreasonable things.

" I'm called Little Buttercup,
   Dear Little Buttercup,
      Though I could never tell why."
[Miss Rosina Brandram in *H.M.S. Pinafore*]

"*And* I'm three-cornered *too*, ain't I?"
[Darrell Fancourt as Dick Deadeye in *H.M.S. Pinafore*]

In an airy tale like this, political and social satire can have very little place. The only references that can be called political even in the remotest sense are those in the final scene, when the Sergeant of Police, having lost the fight against the pirates, calls upon his victorious adversaries to yield in Queen Victoria's name. They yield at once, " because, with all our faults, we love our Queen;" and the nobility of their sentiment affects the policemen to tears. Then Ruth enters and pleads for the pirates on the ground that

> They are no members of the common throng;
> They are all noblemen, who have gone wrong.

This reverses the position at once. Major-General Stanley releases the pirates, tells them to resume their rank and legislative duties, and gives them his daughters as wives, " because, with all our faults, we love our House of Peers."

It may very well be thought that this was mild enough, and nonsensical enough, to pass without hurt feeiings; but Queen Victoria, imbued as she had been by her good but humourless German husband with an immense idea of royal and aristocratic dignity, considered the reference disrespectful.

Other references to topical events and habits are so casual and unemphatic that most of them escape notice altogether while the opera is being performed. For example, the pirates themselves are a parody of a literary fashion. Pirates and picturesque outlaws generally were much in vogue in Gilbert's day. This was the time when J. M. Barrie, at school in Scotland, spent most of his spare time as a member of a pirate band in a garden at Dumfries, and so got some of the material which, 30 years later, he was to turn to good use in *Peter Pan*. It was the time when Stevenson's *Treasure Island* was a new addition to the classics. The Pirate King might be an anachronism, but he was a familiar figure for all that. He conducted his business on romantic rather than practical lines. He failed to make piracy pay, because he

c

was too tender-hearted. As Frederic pointed out, in his last moments before his membership of the band expired, " You make a point of never attacking a weaker party than yourselves, and when you attack a stronger party, you invariably get thrashed."

In the romances of the day, it was usually the weaker party who won (as, indeed, it always is in romances at any time). The Pirate King therefore may be reckoned as topical; and his song, with its introductory remark: " I don't think much of our profession, but, contrasted with respectability, it is comparatively honest," was a shrewd blow at a certain kind of smug hypocrisy which was a fault of the too complacent period in which he was created.

Another shrewd blow, or series of blows, was struck in Major-General Stanley's autobiographical patter-song:

I am the very pattern of a modern Major-General

I've information vegetable, animal and mineral . . .

This song has become famous because of its rattling metre, its amazingly ingenious trisyllabic rhymes, and the opportunities it gives to its singer to show off his ability to speak distinctly at a very high speed. But it is also a critical commentary on the training of the officers in the British Army of that day; and on that subject Gilbert could speak with a certain inside knowledge, for he was himself a keen amateur soldier and was an officer in the Militia, wearing the kilt (curiously enough) of the Gordon Highlanders.

In his usual manner with this type of song, he makes Major-General Stanley reveal—or rather, display with innocent pride—his unsuitability for the high position he occupies. Just as the Judge in *Trial By Jury* states with a calmness verging on complacency that his law is mainly fudge, just as Sir Joseph Porter in *Pinafore* proclaims his lack of acquaintance with the sea, so this highly-educated soldier announces at the end of a tremendous catalogue of accomplishments that he hasn't got "a smattering of elemental strategy."

> For my military knowledge, though I'm plucky
>   and adventury,
> Has only been brought down to the beginning of
>   the century.

We need not enquire too closely here how far Gilbert in this song was making a serious criticism, based on his own experience, of the methods of training in use in the Army, and how far he was merely following his own very successful formula for a topical comic song. It is perhaps relevant to remind ourselves in passing, however, that the Franco-Prussian war, which had shown with startling clarity the efficiency of German military training, was still fresh in men's minds at the time when the song was written. There was in England no fear of possible war with Germany till long after that date, but doubtless there was a feeling that the science of war was not being studied seriously enough in Whitehall.

It is curious to reflect that much of the "useless knowledge which Gilbert laughed at in Major-General Stanley would to-day be considered extremely useful. Consider the first verse of the song:

> I know the kings of England, and I quote the
>   fights historical
> From Marathon to Waterloo, in order categorical;
> I'm very well acquainted, too, with matters
>   mathematical;
> I understand equations, both the simple and
>   quadratical;
> About binomial theorem I'm teeming with a lot
>   o' news
> With many cheerful facts about the square on
>   the hypotenuse.

And he is also " very good at integral and differential calculus." To put it quite simply, he knows military history, without which a really thorough grasp of strategy can hardly be acquired; and he has that head for figures without which no general can hope to cope with a vast modern mechanised scientific battle. In the second verse, his ability to answer hard acrostics marks him as a valuable man with codes and ciphers, while his remark " In conics I can floor peculiarities parabolous " simply means that his higher mathematics are better even than we had thought.

That is by the way, however. Gilbert wrote in the middle of the longest and most profound era of peace that Britain has enjoyed throughout her history, and in the comparatively short time since he wrote war has ceased to be a dangerous form of sport played according to fixed rules by a few initiates. The wonder is that Major-General Stanley's song retains so much of its freshness; and the reason for that is that the precise references in it are not topical, and do not need to be very exactly understood in order to make their effect.

For instance, it is clear enough without explanation that it is not part of an officer's training to " quote in elegiacs all the crimes of Heliogabalus," and the point is not made more striking if you happen to know that Heliogabalus was a Roman Emperor whose excesses led to his assassination in the year A.D. 222. Indeed, as soon as you begin to analyse the song, you find that Gilbert himself did not know (or care) very much about the correctness of his references. If he had, he would not have allowed the line:

> I know our mythic history, King Arthur's and Sir Caradoc's

to be followed soon by:

> And tell you every detail of Caractacus's uniform.

Why? Because, as it happens, Caradoc and Caractacus were

the same person, a historic British chief who fought against the Roman invaders about A.D. 50, and was captured and taken to Rome. His real name was Caradoc, and the Latin equivalent was Caratacus, which has come to be spelt Caractacus. None of this mattered to Gilbert, who in one place was looking for a rhyme to " paradox " and in the other was in need of the name of any ancient soldier whose name would fit neatly into the line. The best way for the modern audience to enjoy this song is to accept its obvious meaning and to avoid concerning itself too deeply with detail.

Throughout this opera there is very little to be found which to an audience of to-day, whether British or American, seems meaningless. The astonishing maidenliness of the General's daughters, who are shocked at the very idea of being seen by a man with their stockings off, was certainly a sign of the Victorian times and rings oddly in the ears of a generation accustomed to seeing all that is to be seen on the bathing beaches of to-day. The chattering chorus, in which the girls talk about the weather while Frederic and Mabel make love, will always have more point here in England, where the weather can never be trusted and is always under discussion, than in America. The extreme respectability of the pirates, whose only idea when they come upon the girls is matrimony, is another Victorian touch.

Mabel's warning to the pirates:

> Hold, monsters! Ere your pirate caravanserai
> Proceed, against our will, to wed us all,
> Just bear in mind that we are wards in Chancery
> And father is a major-general!

calls for explanation. Obviously, since no further reference is made to their legal status and no dramatic use is made of it, Gilbert made the Misses Stanley wards in Chancery merely for the sake of the rhyme with " caravanserai." But two years later, in *Iolanthe,* he was to make much more of this;

69

and I feel little doubt that he did it because he realised that in Mabel's remonstrance to the pirates he had stumbled accidentally on a good idea.

A ward in Chancery, or ward of Court, is a person under 21 years of age who for any reason has come under the protection of the law. Sometimes children are made wards in Chancery in order to save them from bad parents or guardians, but that is obviously not the case in the devoted Stanley family. Any child which is to inherit property of its own when it comes of age automatically becomes a ward of Court if any legal question rises about its property, and probably that is what happened here. A man with sixteen daughters all about the same age might well apply to the Court to be allowed to pay their school bills and dress allowances out of their own money.

The second act of this opera is almost completely devoid of references which call for elucidation. It has been thought by some commentators that the passage in which General Stanley tells Frederic that he has come to humble himself before the tombs of his ancestors is a hit at the rich middle-classes who were retiring to estates in the country. The dialogue runs:

Frederic: But you forget, sir, you only bought the property a year ago, and the stucco in your baronial hall is scarcely dry.

General: Frederic, in this chapel are ancestors: you cannot deny that. With the estate, I bought the chapel and its contents. I don't know whose ancestors they were, but I know whose ancestors they *are*, and I shudder to think that their descendant by purchase (if I may so describe myself) should have brought disgrace upon what, I have no doubt, was an unstained escutcheon.

70

I do not myself believe that Gilbert was here indulging in any kind of social satire. If he had put the speech into the mouth of a man like Sir Joseph Porter, self-confessedly not a gentleman by birth, there might have been good reason to believe that he meant to be acid. But Major-General Stanley, in the absence of any proof to the contrary, must be presumed to be a gentleman by birth, whose escutcheon might be just as impressive as that if the family whose property he had bought. To my mind, Gilbert is here simply amusing himself in his characteristic way, arguing logically from an illogical premise.

The attempt to read into this passage more than Gilbert had intended illustrates a general tendency to make him out a more profound and more deliberate satirist than in fact he was. G. K. Chesterton is the chief offender in this way, for although he makes many illuminating remarks in his scattered comments on Gilbert, and makes them with his accustomed brilliance, he also makes what seems to me the fundamental error of making Gilbert out to be a man deeply dissatisfied with the times he lived in.

I believe the truth to be the exact opposite of this. Gilbert accepted the times he lived in, not certainly as the best possible, but as reasonably good times. If he had not done so, a man with his capacity for blazing indignation would most certainly have indulged it; but in spite of his reputation for blistering comment on events in ordinary life, there is seldom in his writings any real indignation at all. He attempts no reforms, political or social. He merely sees, as the humorist is always privileged to see, that the world is a peculiar place; and he dispassionately points out its peculiarities.

But for all that, the world's peculiarities were not Gilbert's first concern. Before everything else he was a dramatist, a man of the theatre, and his basic need was a theatrically effective situation.

All his satire was incidental to that basic need, and that is why (as Chesterton points out, here making no mistake) all his most telling satire is made by implication rather than direct statement. Chesterton's best instance of this is the song from *Pinafore*, "He is an Englishman." You will remember how this rousing patriotic number goes:

> For he himself has said it,
> And it's greatly to his credit
> That he is an Englishman.
> For he might have been a Rooshian,
> Or French, or Turk, or Prooshian,
> Or perhaps I-tal-i-an.
> Yet in spite of all temptations
> To belong to other nations
> He remains an Englishman!

The solemn absurdity of this would be funny even if it had no particular satirical bite, and still is funny although its immediate topical force has gone. But Chesterton points out that at the time when it was written it was something more than a mere jest. It was a mordant criticism, all the sharper for the casual method of its delivery, of a certain kind of false patriotism. It is true patriotism to be proud of your country and its achievements; but to be proud of yourself because you belong to your country is both foolish and offensive. The fact that Gilbert could see this so clearly at a time when England was on the crest of a great wave of material success shows that he had a quite remarkable detachment of mind.

It was this detachment of mind, coupled with the humorist's delicate sense of proportion, that made a satirist of Gilbert. On all the subjects on which he touched—except one, as I shall point out later—he took the viewpoint of an amused and fairly tolerant outsider. He had no missionary zeal, and no theories; he simply detected anomalies, and made dramatic capital out of them. He seldom took sides, and on occasion the anomalies which he discovered cancelled one another out.

If we try, for instance, to find out what Gilbert really thought about party government, we quickly reach a state of utter confusion. In *H.M.S. Pinafore* he laughs at a system which allows Sir Joseph Porter to rise to Cabinet rank by being a good party man:

> I always voted at my party's call
> And I never thought of thinking for myself at all.
> I thought so little, they rewarded me
> By making me the Ruler of the Queen's Navee.

He comes back to this idea several times in later operas, and in *Utopia Limited* he comes to the conclusion (not precisely stated, but clearly implied) that without party government Britain might well be the ideal State. On the other hand, in *Iolanthe,* he allows the Sentry to voice a very different opinion:

> When in that House M.P.'s divide
>   If they've a brain and cerebellum, too,
> They've got to leave that brain outside
>   And vote just as their leaders tell 'em to.
> But then the prospect of a lot
>   Of dull M.P.'s, in close proximity,
> All thinking for themselves, is what
>   No man can face with equanimity.
>   Then let's rejoice, with loud fal-lal,
>   Fal-lal-la,
>   That nature wisely doth contrive,
>   Fal-lal-la,
>   That every boy and every gal
>   That's born into this world alive
>   Is either a little Liberal
>   Or else a little Conservative,
>   Fal-lal-la.

Clearly, the real case for or against government by party was something on which Gilbert had not really troubled to make up his mind, and the evils which inevitably follow from totalitarian government had never even occurred to him. In the same way, in dealing with social or business matters he is content to point out, as any plain common-sensible layman might, the defects inherent in any system, he is not concerned to invent, or even to advocate, any alternative system. He is not interested in systems, but in their use or abuse by fallible human beings.

CHAPTER VI

" *Patience* "

On April 23rd, 1881, at the Opera Comique, *The Pirates of Penzance* was succeeded by. *Patience, or Bunthorne's Bride,* described as " a new and entirely original aesthetic opera." Much more than any other Gilbert and Sullivan work so far seen, the new piece was a topical satire, for it parodied and laughed to scorn the affectations of an artistic clique. It caught on amazingly, ran for 578 performances, and helped to kill the silly " aesthetic " cult. After that, it might well have been expected to share the fate of other topical satires— to lose its point, to vanish from the stage, and never to be heard by the public again. Instead of that, it has retained its hold on generation after generation of playgoers who neither know nor greatly care what the aesthetes of the 1880's believed or how they behaved.

Nobody could have foreseen that this would happen, but it is plain enough to us, looking back, why it happened. Gilbert, setting out to mock at a passing folly, stumbled on a universal truth. *Patience* still has a meaning for us to-day because it illustrates a conflict that is constantly going on— the conflict between the artist and the plain man. Aestheticism has gone, but all sorts of other -isms have followed in its wake, and each of them has followed the same course. An artist or group of artists reacting against the conventions of the time enunciates a new principle. Lesser artists follow, and a " school " is formed. Lesser artists still imitate the work of the school, carry its principle to exaggerated extremes, and are received with acclamation by half-baked hangers-on. And the plain man, listening to these hangers-on with distaste, dismisses the whole movement as nonsense. Gilbert in

Patience hit off the plain man's attitude so exactly that his opera is still topical. You can still find his Rapturous Maidens in the artistic quarter of any large town—differently dressed, perhaps, and using a different jargon, but easy to recognise, and still pouring out admiration of the " precious nonsense " uttered by the Bunthornes and the Grosvenors of the day.

The " aesthetic " movement at which Gilbert laughed was exactly of the pattern described above, and it originated in the revolt of the Pre-Raphaelite Brotherhood. This was a group of painters, led by Rossetti and backed by Ruskin, the foremost writer of his day on art, which sought relief from the standards of the prosperous, respectable and self-satisfied society of the time in a deliberately cultivated archaism which aimed at being simple but achieved an exaggerated artificiality. The movement was taken up by humourless highbrows who developed aestheticism into a cult not much less foolish or overdone than in Gilbert's parody.

If it had only been the painters who revolted against the standards of the time, it is likely that the aesthetic cult, as such, would never have come into being. Of themselves, those art-lovers among the public who were in sympathy with the Pre-Raphaelites would not have broken out into open extravagance of behaviour; they did so only because they found a leader in Oscar Wilde. This brilliant young man, just down from Oxford, found in the rigidity of Victorian taste a challenge that was not to be resisted. He was a curious compound of poet, wit and exhibitionist, and because he was consistently able to come off best in verbal exchanges he was able to carry off eccentricities of dress and behaviour which amused the iconoclasts, shocked the conventional-minded, and caused many sensible people to dismiss him, quite mistakenly, as a charlatan.

Among those sensible people was Gilbert. Wilde's way of going about in a sort of fancy dress, carrying a flower in his

hand, and talking in picturesque language about Art, was
calculated to rouse the plain man in Gilbert to furious
mockery. It is amusing to reflect how much the two men
had in common below the surface level of their very different
characters. For instance, it is on record that Wilde once
went up to some immensely self-important nonentity who was
making a pompous progress along Piccadilly, tapped him on
the shoulder, and said, " Excuse me, sir, but *are* you anybody in particular?" The tone of the question is almost so
exactly that used by Gilbert in many recorded anecdotes that
we can easily imagine him putting it to Wilde himself if they
had happened to meet. Indeed, one might almost say that
he actually did put this question to Wilde by making him the
original of Reginald Bunthorne, the fleshly poet in *Patience*.

It was fortunate for Gilbert, and for future generations of
playgoers, that he did not lose his temper and make his
caricature of Wilde too personal. Events were to prove that
Wilde, under his mischievous pose, was a serious artist of
considerable importance, and that to have dismissed him
publicly and pointedly as a mere show-off would have made
Gilbert look foolish and have condemned *Patience* to limbo.
As it happened, Gilbert's attack was on the aesthetes in
general and was entirely good-humoured; so that when
Bunthorne confessed himself as a mere poseur—

> Am I alone
>   And unobserved? I am!
> Then let me own
>   I'm an aesthetic sham . . .
> In short, my mediaevalism's affectation
> Born of a morbid love of admiration.

—the words can be taken to apply not necessarily to Wilde
himself, but to any of those among his followers whom they
happen to fit.

Both here and throughout the opera Gilbert makes it quite

clear that he is attacking, not the pre-Raphaelites themselves
—he never mentions them at all—nor even other artists who
came under their influence, but only their foolish followers
who drooped and attitudinised. If the cap fitted Wilde, then
Wilde could wear it; but if it should turn out to be too small
for him, then there were plenty of others whom it did fit.
And it was for the public, not Gilbert, to do the trying-on.

From a letter of his to Sullivan it is clear that the idea of
satirising the aesthetes had been in his mind for some time;
but strangely enough, when he sat down to write *Patience,* it
was not of any kind of artistic charlatan that he was thinking,
but of another even more irritating character of the day, the
sanctimonious young clergyman. In its first draft, *Patience*
was a transference to stage form of Gilbert's Bab Ballad, *The
Rival Curates.* In this poem, the Reverend Clayton Hooper
is a curate so mild and saintly that he is the wonder of the
countryside. One day, however, he hears of another curate,
the Reverend Hopley Porter, who is even milder, more saintly
and more exquisitely effeminate than himself. He sends two
hired assassins to his rival, who threaten him with death
unless he changes his ways.

This is Hopley Porter's answer:

> " What?" said that reverend gent,
>   " Dance through my hours of leisure?
> Smoke? Bathe myself with scent?
>   Play croquet? Oh, with pleasure!
> Wear all my hair in curl?
>   Stand at my door and wink—so—
> At every passing girl?
>   My brothers, I should think so!
> For years I've longed for some
>   Excuse for this convulsion;
> Now that excuse has come—
>   I do it on compulsion."

That is a clear foreshadowing of the climax of *Patience*, when Reginald Bunthorne threatens Archibald Grosvenor with a curse unless he becomes a perfectly commonplace young man. Even the words in which Gosvenor yields are much the same:

Bun: You swear it?

Gros: I do. Cheerfully. I have long wished for a reasonable pretext for such a change as you suggest. Now it has come. I do it on compulsion!

On a foundation of *The Rival Curates*, Gilbert had planned to build up a situation such as Dr. Daly, in *The Sorcerer*, had described in his song " A Pale Young Curate ":

> Time was when love and I were well acquainted,
>> Time was when we walked ever hand in hand,
> A saintly youth, with worldly thought untainted—
>> None better loved than I in all the land!
> Time was when maidens of the noblest station,
>> Forsaking even military men,
> Would gaze upon me, rapt in adoration.
>> Ah me! I was a fair young curate then!

Here is the whole cast of *Patience* in embryo—all but Patience herself, the pretty dairy maid. Here is the chorus of Rapturous Maidens, who in the opera are all still " of the noblest station," for all have titles which show them to be the daughters of dukes, marquises or earls. Here is the chorus of Heavy Dragoons, the military men they have forsaken. Gilbert's course lay clear before him, and he was two-thirds of his way through the libretto, when it occurred to him that to poke quite such elaborate fun at the affectations of the clergy—much though they deserved it—would be certain to cause widespread offence. Rutland Barrington, the actor who played Dr. Daly, had remarked during the rehearsals of *The Sorcerer* that it was a daring innovation to

79

bring a clergyman on to the comic opera stage. The public was very conventional, and very careful of all the outward forms of religion; and silly women ran after parsons (it seems incredible, but it is the fact) much as to-day they run after film-stars. Gilbert decided that his " rival curates " plot was altogether too dangerous, and looked about him for another kind of man who could be satirised in the same way, but with popular approval. And so, he went back to an older notion, and turned his mockery against the aesthetes.

Perhaps it is this very fact, that Gilbert had to change the point of impact of his attack on affectation and foolish hero-worship, that accounts for the survival of *Patience*. A satire intended merely to show up the pretentiousness of the aesthetes might have been so local in its application that it would quickly have become meaningless; the fact that it had to be switched from one form of pretentiousness to another makes it an attack on pretentiousness in general, and gives it universality. Gilbert was not a tolerant man when he found his beliefs questioned, and he believed not only in his age but in himself as an artist. The aesthetes derided the age as vulgar and set up standards of art which could have no validity to Gilbert; and if he had been moved to make a direct attack on Wilde as leader of the movement he might well have said things which time would have proved to be hasty and ill-judged. As things were, he left the leaders alone and contented himself with laughing at their imitators, whom he held up to scorn for self-seeking charlatans. And the methods by which charlatans induce foolish people to admire them for qualities they have not got are much the same in all ages.

When we come to examine the plot of *Patience* in the light of this knowledge, we find that in fact it is much better suited to a pair of curates than to a couple of poets. The first act is set, rather arbitrarily, outside Castle Bunthorne, which stands, we soon learn, outside a country village. Why

Bunthorne lives in such lordly state, and how the twenty love-sick maidens come to be outside his door, and where they spend the rest of their time, and why the whole set of characters are not in St. John's Wood (which was the artistic quarter of London in those days (as Chelsea and Bloomsbury now are) are questions to which no obvious replies offer themselves. But if the castle were a country rectory, and the twenty maidens were the young ladies of the parish, everything becomes at once natural—and so does the fact that the young man on whom all their hearts are set is in love with the village dairy maid. Indeed, it is not till we know that the story originally turned on the tendency of young women in country parishes to dote on curates that we begin to see why the opera lays such emphasis on love. The aesthetes are not concerned with love—not, at any rate, with the ordinary everyday kind of love which ends in marriage. The ladies' competition for the hand of Bunthorne, their habit of following him about in procession and proposing to him in chorus, all make legitimate fun if a saintly young curate is the object of their ministrations but seem a little farfetched as applied to a poet—particularly a poet who, as soon as they leave him alone for a moment, sings a song about quite a different kind of love:

> Then a sentimental passion of a vegetable
>   fashion must excite your languid spleen
> An attachment *á la* Plato for a bashful young
>   potato, or a not-too-French French bean!
> Though the Philistines may jostle, you will rank
>   as an apostle in the high aesthetic band
> If you walk down Piccadilly with a poppy or a
>   lily in your mediaeval hand.
>   And everyone will say
>   As you walk your flowery way,
> " If he's content with a vegetable love which

would certainly not suit me,
Why, what a most particularly pure young
man this pure young man must be!''

That is much more the kind of sentiment to be expected in a skit on self-styled devotees of art, but it is the only number in the whole of the first act which gets away from the theme of love. All the talk about art comes in the dialogue, not the lyrics—except for this one song. The inference is that Gilbert, who always wrote his lyrics first, must have written those for the first act before he decided to drop his curates.

Even in the second act the same slight struggle between the plot and the lyrics continues. It is clear that the duet between Bunthorne and Jane, in which she advises him to compel his rival to become more worldly must have been planned before the change of theme:

Jane: So go to him and say to him, with compliment ironical—

Bun: Sing '' Hey to you,
Good-day to you—''
And that's what I shall say.

Jane: Your style is much too sanctified, your cut is too canonical . . .

These ecclesiastical terms hardly fit Archibald Grosvenor, and (we cannot help thinking) would not have been applied to him if he had not been a curate to begin with. It is true that a line or two later the word '' aesthetic '' comes into the song— but this could easily have been altered, and I am prepared to hazard the guess that Gilbert's original word here was '' ascetic.''

One result of the change of theme is that *Patience* has many fewer topical references than might have been expected. Its concern is still with love rather than art, and the modern audience does not have to have any special knowledge of the aesthetes in order to understand what is going on. A bunch of artistic ladies all in love with a poet, who will have nothing to do with them in that way (though he likes to be admired) because he is in love with a milkmaid—it is the most simple and plain of theatrical situations. Patience herself, with her ignorance of what love is and her growing feeling that it is her duty to find out, is a character who might have stepped out of any Gilbert and Sullivan opera; and it is to be noted that throughout the piece her concern is always with love and never with art at all.

As for the 35th Dragoon Guards, their place in the story is as plain as can be. A year before, they were stationed in the village, and all the ladies were in love with them. Now they come back to their former quarters and expect to be received with the former warmth. Instead, they find that their fiancées have been smitten by a craze for high art, are wearing strange trailing garments and carrying strange musical instruments, and have a perpetual date with an unhealthy-looking poet. Their indignation calls for no explanatory notes.

There must be an explanatory note, however, to the song with which the Colonel introduces himself and them. This, with its rollicking tune, is one of the most famous of Gilbert's songs, and it simply bristles with names and allusions, thrown in at random. The song is complete nonsense, and all it amounts to is that the Heavy Dragoons, in the opinion of their commanding officer, are very fine fellows indeed. He begins:

> If you want a receipt for that popular mystery
>   Known to the world as a Heavy Dragoon,
> Take all the remarkable people in history
>   Rattle them off to a popular tune . . .

And he proceeds to take himself at his word—only the names he rattles off belong not merely to history but to poetry, drama, fiction and the files of contemporary newspapers.

Gilbert's only two objects in this song were to make the list as ridiculous a mixture of incongruous names as he could, and to include as many tricky trisyllabic rhymes as possible. For the purpose of understanding the song it is not necessary to know where all the allusions come from, and I doubt very much if anybody did even in Gilbert's day. When I was at college, a friend with a taste for research set himself to trace them, and succeeded in finding all except one:

The keen penetration of Paddington Pollaky . . .

This reference baffled him completely, and when he left Cambridge he still had not discovered who Paddington Pollaky might be. Since then the Gilbert and Sullivan Society has been formed, and all such mysteries have been solved—and it turns out that Pollaky was an Austrian detective living in the Paddington district of London, who had got his remarkable name into the papers about the time when Gilbert was writing this song.

In order to emphasise my point that the references in the Colonel's song do not need to be understood, I add here a list of elucidations, as full as research can make it, except that I will not insult my readers by explaining Lord Nelson or Bismarck.

Henry Fielding was an English novelist (1707-1754), whose chief work was *Tom Jones.* " Paget about to trepan " was Sir James Paget (1814-1899), a famous surgeon of the day. Jullien, the eminent musico, was a French conductor of no particular lasting note; Lord Macaulay (1800-1859) was author of a famous *History of England;* Dion Boucicault (1822-1890) was an Irish actor and dramatist (already mentioned in a previous chapter). Sodor and Man is the curious name of a diocese in the Church of England which includes the Isle of Man and other smaller islands. D'Orsay was a Parisian dandy who lived in the first half of the 19th century, Dickens and Thackeray explain themselves, and so perhaps does Victor Emanuel, the King of Italy who had died six years before *Patience* was staged.

Peveril was the chief character in Sir Walter Scott's novel *Peveril of the Peak*, Thomas Aquinas a 13th century Italian philosopher, and Doctor Sacheverell an 18th century English divine who got into trouble for preaching political sermons. Tupper was a now forgotten poet of the time whose extraordinary popularity with a public which was impressed by moral sentiments explains his being mentioned in one breath with Tennyson; Defoe an 18th century author of *Robinson Crusoe*, Anthony Trollope a novelist contemporary with Dickens and Thackeray. Monsieur Guizot was a French historian and statesman who died in 1874.

To continue, in detail, hardly seems necessary; but I have committed myself. It is obvious that the whole song is a heterogeneous collection of names known and unknown, but why Lord Waterford was singled out as " reckless and rollicky," and which of various possible Rodericks supplied the swagger, nobody but Gilbert could say. " Sir Garnet " was later Field Marshal Lord Wolseley, Manfred a King of Sicily, The Stranger a character in a play by Kotzebue. " Richardson's Show " was a travelling Barnum-and-Bailey affair, Mr. Micawber (of course) a Dickens character, Madame Tussaud (equally of course) the London waxworks proprietor. And who the Beadle of Burlington was nobody seems to be prepared to say with any authority, though a plausible guess is that the Arcade comes into it somehow.

From this point onwards till quite late in the action there are hardly any topical references except the constantly recurrent parody of the jargon used by the aesthetes; though exactly how far Gilbert was here using the actual vocabulary used by a member of the actual clique and how far he was adding touches of his own is now difficult to establish.

One development of the plot calls for comment, however—
Bunthorne's decision, when Patience refuses him, to put himself up to be raffled for. This is in itself quite a good comic
idea, but as the opera stands it has no very special point—
there is no particular reason why Bunthorne should adopt this
method of settling his fate. The incident was obviously
invented when the subject (or victim) of the raffle was to be
a curate, and in that case it would' have had a very special
rightness. It was one of the odd facts about pious Victorians
that while they abhorred and execrated the sin of gambling
they could see no harm at all in raffles, and used them
constantly as a method of raising money for Church funds or
(as in Bunthorne's case) for deserving charities. As a raffle
is a method of selling something for more than it is worth in
the open market, by distributing tickets to people who take
their chance of drawing the prize, it differs in no essential
way from a sweepstake. Yet a " sweep " was regarded as
a sinful proceeding, while a raffle had about it a heavy
traditional odour of sanctity.

Right at the end of the opera, in the duet between Bunthorne and Grosvenor which begins " When I go out of
door," there is a crop of references almost as long as that in
the Colonel's song, but much more to the point. All the
references here have a purpose—Bunthorne's to emphasise
that he is going to be more aesthetic than ever, Grosvenor that
he is going to be utterly ordinary—" a commonplace type with
a stick and a pipe, and a half-bred black-and-tan." (What,
you ask, is a " black-and-tan "? It was a breed of terrier
much in vogue at the time. Presumably it still exists, though
nobody even seems to mention it in my presence any more.)
This everyday young man works as a Government clerk at
Somerset House, or as a lawyer's clerk in Chancery Lane, or
behind the counter in stores like Sewell and Cross or Howell
and James—firms which were hardly known even in Gilbert's

day and have long since passed out of remembrance. Behind the counter in these establishments he was a " What's the next article?" young man because when he had made a sale his invariable formula was to say to his customer, " And what is the next article I can show you, madam?" Bunthorne's allusions are less factual, and are designed to create a vague atmosphere of " high art " and pre-Raphaelitism rather than to convey any very precise meaning.

Patience has one special claim to notice, for it was the first of what are now often known collectively as the Savoy operas to have a full claim to the title. The fortune which D'Oyly Carte had made out of the early Gilbert and Sullivan works was big enough to enable him to build a fine new theatre as a permanent home for them. When *Patience* had been running for five months and a half at the Opera Comique in Wych Street—neither theatre nor street is now in existence, having been swept away long since in a rebuilding scheme—it had a second and more glittering first night, for the Savoy was the first London theatre to be lit throughout by electricity.

This was on October 10th, 1881. The Prince of Wales was present, and Sullivan conducted; and after the performance, Sullivan took the Prince behind the scenes, to show him the glories of the new building, and to present the principal members of the company to him. The opera had been newly rehearsed and newly dressed for the occasion, and a bigger stage gave room for new recruits to the choruses. Altogether, it was a great day in the theatrical history of London.

CHAPTER VII

"Iolanthe"

Is it mere coincidence that Gilbert, having made a successful fantasy out of one of his ecclesiastical Bab Ballads, should immediately turn to another rhyme of the same kind for a similar purpose?   I have nowhere read anything to prove such a connection between *Patience* and *Iolanthe,* but there is no doubt at all that the new piece, which was produced at the Savoy on November 25th, 1882, was a dramatisation of " The Fairy Curate."

Here is the opening verse of the ballad:

> Once a fairy
> Light and airy
> Married with a mortal;
> Men, however,
> Never, never
> Pass the fairy Portal.
> Slyly stealing,
> She to Ealing
> Made a daily journey;
> There she found him,
> Clients round him
> (He was an attorney).

The whole essence of *Iolanthe* lies in those few lines—the incongruous contrast between the immortal being, for ever young and beautiful on the one hand, and the dry-as-dust lawyer in his respectable suburb on the other.

A son is born to them called George, half a mortal and half a fairy. He grows up and becomes a clergyman. Then one day, when his mother happens to be paying him a visit, the Bishop walks in:

88

" Who is this, sir—
Ballet miss, sir?"
Said the Bishop coldly.
" 'Tis my mother,
And no other,"
Georgie answered boldly.
" Go along, sir!
You are wrong, sir.
You have years in plenty;
While this hussy
(Gracious mussy!)
Isn't two-and-twenty!"

(Fairies clever
Never, never
Grow in visage older,
And the fairy
All unwary
Leant upon his shoulder.)
Bishop grieved him,
Disbelieved him,
George the point grew warm on;
Changed religion
Like a pigeon*
And became a Mormon.

* " Like a bird."

(This reference to the pigeon, and its explanatory footnote, is a perfect example of the way in which a joke which
is obvious to its own generation can be quite meaningless to
later ages. In 1882 and for many years afterwards, " like a
bird " was a common catch-phrase expressing willingness.
" I'll do it like a bird " meant " I'll fly to do it." It was as

common, and meant very much the same, as " O.K., chief!" in our time.)

Change the curate, as before, into a layman; allow him to be found with the fairy in his arms, not by the Bishop but by the lady of his love—and the main part of the plot of *Iolanthe* is complete. Next, perhaps, came the happy thought of making the lovers a pair of powder-and-patch Arcadians such as, in Dresden china, adorned half the mantelpieces in London. Then the choruses. The women would obviously be fairies—but the men? Promote George's father, the attorney of the poem, to the highest rank that a lawyer can hold in England—make him Lord Chancellor. Then he will be the leader of the House of Lords, and the men's chorus will be peers, gorgeous in coronets and ceremonial robes. Use the idea from the poem, also, that Georgie's mother employed her fairy gifts to help her son's interests, answering the questions in his examinations and so on. Make the fairies send the Arcadian shepherd into Parliament, set the second act in Palace Yard, Westminster, and the whole affair will be an enchanting contrast of fantasy and matter-of-factness. In some such way Gilbert's thoughts may have run, for he must have realised that these events and characters gave his special talents every chance. He was at home in fairyland, and fairies, as we have seen already, were in fashion. He was a lawyer, and loved legal quibbles. He was always happy poking fun at the absurdities of established institutions which at heart he deeply respected, and among such institutions the House of Lords stood high.

At the time when Gilbert was writing the House of Lords had reached a midway stage in the long story of its evolution. It is one of the best examples that can be brought forward of the traditional British way of keeping the form of an outworn institution, but changing its content to suit the altered times. The peers, during the early history of Britain, were a powerful group of nobles who, under a still more powerful king, ruled the country for their own benefit. (The word " peer " means " an equal," and its meaning of a representative nobleman came from Charlemagne, who appointed twelve peers to help him govern, so called because they were all equal in power.) Much later, when England curbed the power of its kings and became a democracy, the House of Commons became responsible for governing the country, while that of the Lords became a hereditary second chamber with an effective power of veto but not much more. To-day, it has less power still and can hardly be called even a hereditary body; for it is now the custom to raise to the peerage men who have distinguished themselves in every walk of life. These newcomers have turned the Upper Chamber into an extremely efficient advisory body, artistocratic in form but surprisingly democratic in temper.

In Gilbert's day this last stage was not yet in sight. The House of Lords was still much as it had been in the 18th century, a collection of aristocrats who thought, and were encouraged on all hands to go on thinking, that high birth was in itself a complete and sufficient claim to privilege. As a body they had no great power to direct events, but individually those of them who wished to do so could wield enormous influence. Most of the wealth of the country was in their hands, and socially they were paramount. It was a comparatively rare thing in those days for a peerage to be conferred on anybody who was not already by birth and up-bringing a member of the upper class, except certain prominent lawyers, who had to be in the House of Lords *ex officio*.

It was well known (indeed, it was a standing joke) that a very large proportion of the heads of noble families with seats in the House seldom or never troubled to occupy those seats. Many of these " backwoodsmen " entrenched themselves in their country houses and could hardly be enticed up to London on any pretext whatever. They administered their estates, they took part sometimes in local government, they hunted, shot and fished in due season, they bred horses, cattle and pigs, and they left politics to the politically-minded. But if the House of Commons tried to pass some measure of which they disapproved, they were quite capable of appearing in the House of Lords in a shocked phalanx and throwing that measure out. For this reason, there was talk of reform—but the Lords still were an institution as solid as the Army, the Navy or the law, and Gilbert could laugh at their absurdities with disrespectful affection and with perfect assurance that everybody would know he was merely jesting.

Iolanthe is an excellent example of Gilbert's craftsmanship. The speed with which it gets off the mark, once the Chorus of Fairies has entered the Arcadian landscape and introduced itself, is quite admirable. In a very short time the whole of the complicated and fantastic situation is made clear to the audience—Iolanthe's crime in marrying a mortal, her death-sentence commuted to penal servitude for life, her pardon, the existence of her son Strephon the Arcadian shepherd, half-mortal half-fairy, his engagement to Phyllis, the Arcadian shepherdess who is also a ward in chancery, Strephon's inability to get the Lord Chancellor's consent to their marriage, and the Fairy Queen's suggestion that she might help him to get into Parliament. Not a moment is wasted in getting all this across the footlights, and stroke follows stroke of the characteristic Gilbertian humour, each rising logically out of the other.

Only one real dramatic slip does Gilbert make, when he allows one of the three chief fairies, Leila, to say to another, Celia:

> That sentence of penal servitude she is now working out, on her head, at the bottom of that stream.

"Iolanthe"

There is a double lapse here. First, Celia has already shown in the preceding dialogue that she knows as much about Iolanthe's punishment as Leila does; it is a very elementary rule for young dramatists that it is bad writing to let one character tell another character something that both already know, merely because the author wants the audience to know it. Second " on her head " is a feeble dragged-in joke which cannot have got much of a laugh at any time and is now without a point. In Gilbert's time to say that a person could do an allotted task " on his head " meant that he could do it easily. The phrase still is heard from time to time, but not so often; and the suggestion that Iolanthe is actually upside-down at the bottom of her stream seems merely unnecessary.

Of a very different order is Strephon's account of his application to the Lord Chancellor:

> To all my tearful prayers he answers me, " A shepherd lad is no fit helpmate for a ward of Chancery." I stood in court, and there I sang him songs of Arcadee, with flageolet accompaniment—in vain. At first he seemed amused, so did the Bar; but quickly wearying of my song and pipe, bade me get out. A servile usher, then, in crumpled bands and rusty bombazine, led me, still singing, into Chancery Lane! I'll go no more! I'll marry her to-day, and brave the upshot, be it what it may!

This absurd picture is not only funny in itself, but it sets the tone of the rest of the opera. Up to this point, we have been concerned with fairyland only, but Strephon gives us the first hint that the fairies are coming to London and are going to mix themselves up with the law and the government, and that the world of fantasy is going to be superimposed on the matter-of-fact world with most surprising results.

93

In himself, Strephon is a stock Gilbertian character. Like his predecessors, Ralph Rackstraw the able seaman and Frederic the pirate apprentice, he is a young man of humble position and (presumably) no education who speaks in flowing periods that would not disgrace an archbishop. When the Fairy Queen says, " Let me see, I've a borough or two at my disposal. Would you like to go into Parliament?" we cannot help feeling that she has hit on exactly the right career for one with such a gift of language.

(Incidentally, the Queen's remark that she has " a borough or two " at her disposal needs explanation, for it is a reference to a state of affairs which was fresh in the memories of Gilbert's contemporaries, but is now part of ancient and forgotten history. The House of Commons is, and in theory always has been, an elected body. At first, however, there was no settled and general rule about the franchise, and the right to vote was conferred very differently in different parts of the country, and particularly in the boroughs. This led gradually to all kinds of abuses. Some boroughs with large populations and long lists of potential voters had no representation in Parliament at all, others with hardly any voters had the right of returning several members. Constituencies which had decayed—" rotten boroughs " as they were called—gradually ceased to be electoral in any but an academic sense. They often fell into the hands of influential people, were regarded by them as personal property, and were actually bought and sold. About the end of the 18th century a very large proportion of the Members of Parliament were nominees of these powerful vested interests, which were in fact so powerful that they effectually prevented the reforms which were being constantly advocated. In 1832, however, the Reform Bill was triumphantly passed into law, and the rotten boroughs with next to no voters, and the pocket boroughs which had become private property, were all legislated out of existence.)

This remark of the Fairy Queen's, therefore, dates *Iolanthe* as happening before 1830. This brings it into line with *H.M.S. Pinafore,* which belonged, like all Gilbert's rhymes and stories of the sea, to the old Navy of masts and sails. Sir Joseph Porter, it may be remembered, certainly got into Parliament in pre-reform days, for he says:

> I grew so rich that I was sent
> By a pocket borough into Parliament . . .

So far as the gift of language is concerned, Phyllis is Strephon's exact female counterpart. Like him—and, for that matter, like Patience the milkmaid—she combines low birth with a high-bred vocabulary. Indeed, she is so very ladylike in all her ways that it comes as a shock to hear her say of herself in song a little later, " My behaviour is rustic but hearty." Patience might possibly have said something of the sort and have carried conviction, for there is evidence that she did actually work in a dairy; but shepherdess Phyllis shows no sign of ever having seen a sheep. She is the kind of shepherdess that Marie Antoinette and her ladies liked to pretend to be, and it is no surprise to find her on easy terms with the aristocracy.

When Strephon urges her to marry him at once because half the House of Lords are sighing at her feet, she merely remarks, " The House of Lords are certainly extremely attentive," taking for granted that it should be so. " Why," Strephon demands, " did five-and-twenty Liberal Peers come down to shoot over your grass-plot last autumn? It couldn't have been the sparrows. Why did five-and-twenty Conservative Peers come down to fish your pond? It couldn't have been the gold-fish!" Gilbert is here taking the chance of a sly dig at the habit of the English gentry of his day of treating every visit to the country as an excuse for killing things; but that incidental touch about the gold-fish finally disposes of Phyllis's claim to be treated as a simple peasant. That fable perhaps may serve her turn as well as any other, but we need not believe that she is anything but a piece of Dresden china come to life.

After the lovers have had their short scene together, the stage is left empty for one of the most effective entrances that Gilbert ever contrived, that of the procession of Peers. As an essay in the mock-heroic it cannot easily be surpassed—yet here again is a joke the full quality of which must, I imagine, be tasted only by an English audience. As each of these superbly robed and coronetted figures paces solemnly on to the stage, the sense of absurdity, for those who know that never in any but the most formidably formal occasion would any member of the House of Lords consent to appear in public dressed like that, is multiplied. For an audience which is not quite sure on this point, half the joke is lost. It is on record that when *Iolanthe* first appeared in New York (which it did simultaneously with the London opening, so far as the difference in sun-time would allow) anxious enquiries were made whether this was, in fact, the garb in which the British aristocracy took its walks abroad. For modern audiences outside Britain it might seem quite natural to suppose that in 1880 noblemen did go about like that.

Yet even for spectators who are not quite sure where reality ends and burlesque begins, the sight of these magnificent personages, before whom the masses, the tradesmen, and the lower middle classes are called on to bow the knee, marching in to their own imitation of the sounds of trumpets and cymbals, is irresistibly comic. And when they are followed on to the stage by the Lord Chancellor, in *his* less colourful but equally dignified official robes and a full-bottomed wig—both of which he continues to wear throughout the play, so that the man is never separated in our

" We look over it."
[Darrell Fancourt and Martyn Green as the Pirate King
and Major-General Stanley in *The Pirates of Penzance*]

" Lovesick all against our will."
[Joan Gillinham as Lady Angela, Joyce Wright as
Lady Saphir, Muriel Harding as Lady Ella in *Patience*]

minds from his office—disrespect reaches its ultimate height.

Officially, there is no greater figure in England, except for Royalty itself, than the Lord High Chancellor. Occupying his historic seat, the Woolsack, he acts as chairman of the House of Lords and is its chief judicial officer. He presides over the Court of Chancery, an austere and remote citadel of justice where matters are decided not by juries of ordinary citizens but by lawyers in solemn argument. Though this tribunal is not presented on the stage in *Iolanthe,* Gilbert gradually builds up in our imagination a travesty of its proceedings as wild as that of an ordinary court in *Trial By Jury*. I have referred already to Strephon's appearance in court with song and flageolet accompaniment; but Strephon is not the only musician heard there. The Lord Chancellor himself sets the fashion. Lord Mountararat is our witness here :

> His Lordship is constitutionally as blithe as a bird—
> he trills upon the bench like a thing of song and
> gladness. His series of judgments in F sharp, given
> *andante* in six-eight time, are among the most
> remarkable effects ever produced in a Court of
> Chancery. He is perhaps the only living instance
> of a judge whose decrees have received the honour
> of a double encore.

All of a piece with this airy nonsense is the picture of that solemn court as a place where pretty young girls attend in a chattering crowd to have their futures settled for them by the Chancellor in person, while he is attracted to them all in turn, like his colleague and forerunner, the Judge in *Trial By Jury* :

> And every one who'd marry a ward
> Must come to me for my accord,
> And in my court I sit all day,

> Giving agreeable girls away,
> With one for him—and one for he—
> With one for you—and one for ye—
> And one for thou—and one for thee—
> But never, oh never a one for me!
> Which is exasperating for
> A highy susceptible Chancellor!

And now at last one of the agreeable wards has tried his susceptibilities too far. Phyllis has brought all the bachelors in the House of Lords to such a pitch of amorousness that they have applied to the Lord Chancellor in a body to ask him to award her hand to the most deserving— and he wants her for himself. It is this last stroke that gives Gilbert one of the best chances of being Gilbertian. In some of the earlier operas we have seen how strongly he was attracted to a situation in which a character's sense of official duty makes him act against his personal desires. There is a suggestion of this situation in John Wellington Wells's death, but it is not fully worked out. In the *Pirates,* however, it is the motive force of the whole story, and in *Patience* there is more than a touch of it. Frederic is forced by his sense of the sacred nature of his indentures to perform all kinds of distasteful duties, and Patience engages herself to the wrong man purely because she has got it into her head that true love must be unselfish. All these characters were, however, private individuals with nothing but their own consciences to satisfy. In the Lord Chancellor we have the spectacle of a public official in the same sort of dilemma. Here is his own description:

> " The feelings of a Lord Chancellor in love with
> a ward of Court are not to be envied. What is his
> position? Can he give his own consent to his own
> marriage with his own ward? Can he marry his
> own ward without his own consent? And if he

marries his own ward without his own consent, can
he commit himself for contempt of his own Court?
And if he commit himself for contempt of his own
Court, can he appear by counsel before himself, to
move for arrest of his judgment? Ah, my Lords,
it is indeed painful to have to sit upon a woolsack
which is stuffed with such thorns as these!"

How far the actual members of the House of Lords
enjoyed seeing themselves and their august leader thus
reduced to figures of fun depended on each man's individual
ability to take a laugh against himself. No doubt some
pompous persons were offended by the constant insistence
on the lack of brains in the peerage, but this, after all, was
an old and popular joke, and there was no real bite in
Gilbert's satire. When he suggested various reforms that
Strephon would be able to make with the assistance of the
Fairy Queen, he probably had no idea at all that any
of his words would come true. At the time when he wrote,
the only two parties in existence were the Conservatives (or
Tories) and the Liberals; the Labour Party, with its
socialistic ideals, had yet to win a single seat in the Commons.
That a new factor in politics was shortly to come into operation, and eventually into power, was a possibility which had .
never occurred to Gilbert, or to the Fairy Queen, or to the
Sentry who in the second act was to stand on guard outside
the House of Lords and sing his still famous but now
completely outdated refrain:

> I often think it's comical—fal, lal, la!
> How Nature always does contrive—fal, lal, la!
>> That every boy and every gal
>>> That's born into this world alive
>> Is either a little Liberal,
>>> Or else a little Conservative!
>>>> Fal, lal, la!

Consequently, the fearful threats which the Fairy Queen utters sound very feeble to modern ears. She tells the Lords that they shall sit, if Strephon sees reason, through the grouse and salmon season; that he will end the cherished rights (whatever they were—no, don't tell me) that the House enjoyed on Wednesday nights; that he will " prick that annual blister, Marriage with deceased wife's sister "—a measure long since passed into law; that he will flood the House with new titles (which has since been done). Only her final threat, of throwing dukedoms open to competitive examination, still sounds extravagant to us; and as for suggesting, as many now suggest, that the House of Lords should be superseded by an elected Second Chamber, she never came within hail of such a revolutionary idea.

The political side of *Iolanthe* therefore belongs to the past, and most of its social references have " dated " similarly. They are not of paramount importance—but it may be of interest if I make some marginal comments on such of them as I have not already mentioned.

First in order, then, comes Phyllis's rejection of her noble suitors. Gilbert was always ready to make fun of stock theatrical situations and ideas, and one of his favourites was the notion, not by any means confined to the English theatre, that the poor were on the whole good and the rich on the whole wicked. In our time this is a political idea, held with fervour by some Socialists and with blind passion by all Communists. In Gilbert's day it was part of the social cant which happened to be in fashion. Phyllis, then, was not content merely to refuse the offered hands and hearts of the aristocracy—she must make an issue of it:

> Nay, tempt me not,
> To rank I'll not be bound;
> In lowly cot
> Alone is virtue found!

This leads to a protest by the Chorus:

> Nay, do not shrink from us, we will not hurt you—
> The Peerage is not destitute of virtue.

And this protest is elaborated by Lord Tolloller in the ballad "Spurn not the nobly born," with its beautifully pointed climax:

> Hearts just as pure and fair
> May beat in Belgrave Square
> As in the lowly air
> Of Seven Dials!

These words struck right home, for Seven Dials, to-day a dingy but harmless London neighbourhood, was then a notorious haunt of criminals.

In the long finale to the first act there is little that needs interpretation. This passage is worth close attention, however, on the part of all who want examples of Gilbert's work at its highest point of skill. The whole of the complicated network of misunderstandings which is caused by Iolanthe's youthful appearance is told in verse so clear that it might be prose dialogue and so varied that it inspires Sullivan to some of his happiest work. Perhaps a note is necessary, in passing, on the use of foreign words—*Repente, Dolce far niente, Festina Lente, Canaille, Plebs, Hoi Polloi*. Gilbert, as we know, always took a mischievous delight in ingenious rhyming, and in certain moods he seemed to be the better pleased the more far-fetched these rhymes were.

Every one of the foreign words and phrases quoted above was in fact used to get a rhyme, and no doubt the first three were dragged in partly because without them the writer could not have found as many rhymes for "five-and-twenty" as his scheme called for. But they have all another justification —they are perfectly in character. Gilbert may allow his peers to laugh at themselves as being people of no special brain-power; but he could rely on the fact that in those days what was specifically called " the education of a gentleman " was based solidly on the classics, Latin and Greek, and included at least a smattering of French. In addition to this, Latin was the language of the law, and the Lord Chancellor was just the man to express himself with the aid of a classical tag:

> Recollect yourself, I pray,
> And be careful what you say—
> As the ancient Romans said, *festina lente*
> For I really do not see
> How so young a girl could be
> The mother of a man of five-and-twenty.

While as for the fairies, it is part of Gilbert's assumption that they are practically omniscient beings, with brains of a specially high order. Consequently, when the Peers make haughty references to the common people in those three languages, it is quite in order for the fairies to comment as they go along:

Peers:	Our lordly style
	You shall not quench
	With base *canaille*!
Fairies:	(That word is French.)
Peers:	Distinction ebbs
	Before a herd
	Of vulgar *plebs*.
Fairies:	(A Latin word.)
Peers:	'Twill fill with joy
	And madness stark
	The οἱ πολλοι!
Fairies:	(A Greek remark.)

The second act begins with the Sentry's song, already mentioned. We learn his identity a little later.

"Iolanthe"

Queen: Who are you, sir?
Sentry: Private Willis, B. Company, 1st Grenadier Guards.
Queen: You're a very fine fellow, sir.
Sentry: I'm generally admired.

A purist has pointed out that the Guards regiments do not in fact do sentry duty in Palace Yard, and has suggested that Gilbert, usually so meticulously correct in naval and military matters, has made a slip. The point is not of great importance, but my own feeling is that the " slip " was deliberate. Gilbert needed a Guardsman, specially selected for his fine physique, in order that the Fairy Queen's confession, " If I yielded to a natural impulse I should fall down and worship that man," might have more point, and by a pardonable dramatic licence he took a Guardsman.

Lord Mountararat's song early in this act is perhaps the best-known example of Gilbert's way of making his characters glory in their own deficiencies. It has all the outward appearance of a glowing eulogy, with its initial flourish:

> When Britain really ruled the waves
>   (In good Queen Bess's time)

but all it in fact says is that Britain has always got on best when the Second Chamber has kept its fingers out of the pie. The last verse rams this point home:

> And while the House of Peers withholds
>   Its legislative hand,
> And noble statesmen do not itch
> To interfere in matters which
>   They do not understand,
> As bright will shine Great Britain's rays
> As in King George's glorious days!

How much, I wonder, does the Lord Chancellor's nightmare song need annotation? It is perhaps the most famous of all Gilbert's patter songs, and it depends for its effect not

103

on any topical allusions or local names, but on its intricate metre and the impression it gives of the growing horror of a sleepless night. Does any American audience listen to it with any keener appreciation for being reminded that Harwich is a port on the east coast of England, that second-class carriages used to exist on all our railways but are now found (I believe) only on expresses to the Continent, that Sloane Square and South Kensington are adjacent stations on the oldest of London's underground railways, that a four-wheeler is a horse-drawn cab, or that Rothschild and Baring were famous financial firms? I am sure that it does not, and will therefore refrain from further elaboration. Nor do I feel that any explanation need be offered of the trio, " Faint heart never won fair lady," which is simply a rendering into verse of a string of popular proverbs and sayings, most of which are familiar to everybody, but some of which are obscure in the extreme.

Enough has already been said, also, to point the Lord Chancellor's description of the success of his efforts to persuade himself to consent to his own marriage with his own ward. This leads to Iolanthe's appeal on behalf of her son, and, when this fails, to her admission that she is the Lord Chancellor's long-lost fairy bride; and so in turn to the Queen's dilemma when she finds that all the fairies have married peers and all are liable to the death-penalty—and to the delightful denouement when all the mortal characters are turned into fairies.

Before leaving this opera, however, I should like to call attention to three jests which depended entirely on contemporary knowledge, and have lost meaning to-day except for archaeologists.

Two of them are trivial enough. At the beginning of Act II, Lord Mountararat says of Strephon's success in Parliament, " He's a parliamentary Pickford—he carries everything!" The firm of Pickford, which still is a leader in the furniture-removing industry, used to have a slogan plastered on hoardings everywhere "Pickford Carries Everything."

Again, later in the act, Phyllis after her reconciliation with Strephon, says to him, " But does your mother know you're . . . I mean, is she aware of an engagement?" This is a reference to a catch-word familiar in London, which was used to imply lack of sophistication, and ran, " Does your mother know you're out?"

The third is more elaborate. It is the Fairy Queen's reference to Captain Shaw in the song in which she admits her love for Private Willis, but declares that she will never give way to it. Here is the second verse of the song:

> On fire that glows
>   With heat intense
> I turn the hose
>   Of common-sense
> And out it goes
>   At small expense!
> We must maintain
>   Our fairy law;
> That is the main
>   On which to draw—
> In that we gain
>   A Captain Shaw!
> (*Aside*) Oh, Captain Shaw
>   Type of true love kept under!
>   Could thy Brigade
>   With cold cascade
>   Quench my great love, I wonder?

The whole verse carries on the metaphor of a fire-brigade, and the head of London's fire brigade when the song was first sung was a Captain Shaw. He was a man-about-town and a regular first-nighter, and was present (as, of course, Gilbert expected him to be) at the opening performance of *Iolanthe*. There was a great roar of delight from the audience at the idea that he typified " true love kept under," and the officer found himself embarrassed and gratified at his unexpected moment of fame. He would have been startled indeed if he had known how often that moment was to recur, and to how many generations his name was to be familiar.

CHAPTER VIII

"Princess Ida" and "The Mikado"

When Gilbert put into the mouth of the Fairy Queen the four
lines which I quoted in the last chapter:

> On fire which glows
> With heat intense
> I turn the hose
> Of common-sense

he might well have been describing his own method as a
satirist. Common-sense was the essential quality of his mind.
The fire of indignation whose intense heat inflames the thought
of fiercer writers died down in his mind to a temperate
warmth. It was this quality that enabled him to laugh at
the absurdities of an institution without losing his respect for
it; and it accounts therefore for his good temper and for his
long survival. The indignation of the reformers served its
purpose and burnt itself out, the cheerful glow and crackle
of Gilbert's mockery still remains.

This statement is self-evidently true and can hardly be
called in question. And yet, how can we reconcile it with
another statement, also generally accepted, that Gilbert was
a sentimentalist? Common-sense implies cool control of the
emotions, while sentimentality is a surrender to easy and
shallow emotions. How can the two exist in the same man?

The answer as I see it is that Gilbert confined his sentimentality to his feelings about women. On all other subjects
he was able to be cool, detached and sensible; but he looked
at women through a romantic haze. If they were young,
lovely, and useless he was ready to worship them, but if they
stepped off the pedestal he was equally ready to punish them

with harsh gibes for their failure to live up to his ideal. He has no sympathy for the rich attorney's elderly, ugly daughter in *Trial By Jury,* or for cousin Hebe in *Pinafore,* or Ruth in *The Pirates of Penzance,* or Lady Jane in *Patience.* His unfeeling attitude towards the ageing unmarried woman has been said often enough to show a streak of cruelty in his nature, but I think this is to overstate the case. Gilbert's attitude towards women was that of the typical Victorian father of a family, and his feeling towards this particular stock character was not so much cruelty as the exasperation of a father towards an unattractive daughter who will not accept the fact that she is unmarriageable, but goes on setting her cap at the men and making a fool of herself. This aspect of his character constantly impresses itself. Though he had no children of his own, he constituted himself a fierce pater-familias to the young women of the Savoy Theatre, principals and chorus alike. It is on record that one group of young men in the audience who had sent a note round to the stage door inviting Jessie Bond, the soubrette of the company, to supper after the show found themselves confronted instead by a tall furious man who ordered them out of the theatre in the approved style of the outraged Victorian parent.

To feel like this about women is to be opposed, auto-matically and inexorably, to any movement for their emancipation. If woman is to be little more than an ornament to life, a pet and plaything for the dominant male, it stands to reason that it is mere waste of time to educate her above her station. That Gilbert believed this with fervour is seen from the effect on him of Tennyson's poem, " The Princess."

The princess of that poem withdrew herself from the world, and founded a university—a self-sufficient community of women. Tennyson's approving picture of " sweet girl-graduates with their golden hair " excited Gilbert to such a pitch that he made, in 1870, what he called " a respectful perversion " of the poet's work. It may have been respectful to Tennyson, but it certainly was not respectful to the girl graduates, for it not merely poured scorn on those advanced feminists who believed that women, once emancipated, would prove to be man's intellectual superior; it went further and denied that women had any aptitude for or claim to higher education at all. So strong was Gilbert's prejudice against women's colleges that in 1884, fourteen years after its first appearance, he thought it a good idea to turn his Tennysonian parody into the libretto of an opera. And so *Princess Ida or Castle Adamant* came into being.

Gilbert had written his parody in blank verse, and in five scenes. In making his new musical version he not only kept the blank verse form but actually transferred long passages of dialogue from one composition to the other, and he followed the dramatic construction of the original as far as possible, turning the five scenes into three acts instead of the usual two. This innovation was forced on him because only the first of the five scenes was set in King Hildebrand's country, the other four passing at Castle Adamant. This first scene, with its dialogue cut a little to allow the songs to be inserted, provided Gilbert with a ready-made opening act, a little on the short side; after which the only way of keeping the whole in equilibrium was to compress the other four scenes into two acts of similar length. *Princess Ida* was produced at the Savoy on January 5th, 1884, and was so well received that it seemed likely to rival its immediate prede-cessors in length of run. In the result, however, it fell far short of them, and was taken off after 246 performances—a very minor success, by Savoy standards.

Gilbert's lyrics and Sullivan's music for this opera were above rather than below their own extraordinary high average, and it seems clear that the reason for the public's lack of real enthusiasm was the story itself, or rather the mixture of prejudice and bad temper which Gilbert had shown in telling it. For once, he had been unable to turn on the hose of common-sense, and as a result he found himself in opposition to all but the most obstinately unprogressive sections of opinion. Higher education for women was making such strides in the third quarter of the 19th century that the rather elementary sneers of *Princess Ida* seemed cheap and foolish.

Gilbert's attitude is crystallised in the number given to Hilarion, Cyril and Florian in Act 2, when they have climbed the wall of Castle Adamant:

Florian : A woman's college! maddest folly going!
What can girls learn within its walls worth knowing?
I'll lay a crown (the Princess shall decide it)
I'll teach them twice as much in half an hour outside it.

Hilarion : Hush, scoffer; ere you sound your puny thunder
List to their aims and bow your head in wonder!

Hilarion : They intend to send a wire
To the moon—to the moon,
And they'll set the Thames on fire
Very soon—very soon;
Then they learn to make silk purses
With their rigs—with their rigs
From the ears of Lady Circe's
Piggy wigs—piggy wiggs.
And weasels at their slumbers
They trepan—they trepan;
To get sunbeams from cu*cum*bers
They've a plan—they've a plan.
They've a firmly rooted notion
They can cross the Polar Ocean,
And they'll find Perpetual Motion
If they can—if they can.

There is a lovely lilt to this lyric (and Sullivan set it most charmingly) but there is prejudiced scorn in every line of it. It is a piled-up list of proverbs and parables of wasted effort and scientific pipe-dreams. Cyril follows with a second verse in the same tone:

> As for fashion, they foreswear it
> So they say—so they say—
> And the circle they will square it
> Some fine day—some fine day.
> Then the little pigs they're teaching
> For to fly—for to fly;
> And the niggers they'll be bleaching
> By-and-by—by-and-by.
> Each newly joined aspirant
> To the clan—to the clan—
> Must repudiate the tyrant
> Known as Man—known as Man—
> They mock at him and flout him
> For they do not care about him
> And they're going to do without him
> If they can—if they can!

Lightly and brilliantly though this is put, there is rancour here—the wounded vanity of the dominant Victorian male who sees his domination threatened; the shocked propriety of the sentimentalist who believes that a woman can develop her intellect only at the expense of her womanliness. In holding these beliefs Gilbert was behind his time. *Princess Ida* was slightly out-of-date when it was written, and became hopelessly out-of-date as soon as public opinion had accepted the idea that some women at least ought to have the same educational opportunities as men.

Time and two world wars have also conspired to make utter nonsense of Gilbert's last act. King Hildebrand, having been defied by Princess Ida, lays siege to her castle. The garrison of girls, outwardly brave in their armour but secretly frightened to death, appear with battle-axes. The Princess inquires with asperity where their rifles are, and is answered:

> Why, please you, ma'am
> We left them in the armoury, for fear
> That in the heat and turmoil of the fight
> They might go off!

To theatre audiences who know how bravely women can stand up to bombardment—not only the trained young woman of the modern auxiliary forces, but delicately-nurtured old ladies who were girls in Gilbert's day—the way in which Princess Ida's entire community deserts her at the first threat of real danger is a very poor joke indeed.

When *Princess Ida* finished its run, no new opera was ready to take its place. This was not entirely because the collaborators had not had time to think out what the successor was to be, but because they had had their first disagreement. Sullivan had been knighted in 1883, and had been listening to those of his friends who told him that writing light music to Gilbert's rhymes was beneath his new dignity. He was making, and spending, too much money to wish to break the partnership, but he did begin to demand a libretto which would give his music more scope. Gilbert, who knew much better than Sullivan where the strength and the potential weaknesses of the partnership lay, was not impressed by any need for change. Also, he had a problem of his own to solve. With *Princes Ida* he had used up the last of his previous writings which could be turned into comic opera, and for the future he must look about him for new ideas; and these do not come to a writer of 47 as easily as to a youth. He had one idea in his head which he thought would do—a plot based on a lozenge which would make anybody who swallowed it become in reality what he pretended to be. It was a good Gilbertian notion, but Sullivan did not like it. He wanted to get away from impossible or supernatural effects, and said so. Gilbert had no other suggestion to make, and thought Sullivan's objection capricious and arbitrary. At one point Sullivan said that he was not going on writing Savoy opera at all, and had to be reminded by the horrified Carte that he was bound by a recent five-year contract to do so when called on. At last, when affairs had reached an unhappy state of deadlock, Gilbert had another idea—which came to him, it is said, when he was looking at a Japanese sword hanging on a wall. Sullivan was so delighted to hear that the new piece was to have no magic in it that he agreed to set it without asking what it was. Gilbert settled down to write *The Mikado* in the second half of 1884; and as by that time *Princess Ida* was beginning to flag, Carte filled in the gap by reviving *Trial By Jury* and *The Sorcerer,* which ran for 150 performances and tided the theatre over until the new piece arrived, which it did on March 15th, 1885.

The Mikado is by common consent the Gilbert and Sullivan chef d'oeuvre. As so often happens after a quarrel has been made up, both partners came to their work with a new freshness of attack. The setting of the play was both picturesque and popular, for Japan, the first nation of the Far East to imitate Western progress, was a kind of fashionable new toy to London society. Gilbert had already glanced at this when he made Bunthorne, in *Patience,* confess:

> I am *not* fond of all one sees
> That's Japanese . . .

and in 1885 there was a Japanese Exhibition being held in London, from which Gilbert, thorough as ever, obtained authentic first-hand information and coaching for his company about Japanese manners, customs and dress.

As the actual Mikado of Japan was regarded by his subjects as a divine being, it is not surprising that the

Japanese Ambassador of the day objected to the piece on the ground that it brought his ruler into ridicule. The protest was not upheld, because it was obvious (to Englishmen, anyhow) that Gilbert had had no thought of the real Mikado or the real Japan in his head. The Japan of the opera was just a Gilbertian topsy-turvydom. Still, the references to boiling oil, decapitation, the "happy despatch," and other drastic Oriental punishment cannot have pleased the Japanese very much; and in 1907 a similar protest actually did lead to the banning of a proposed revival of the opera.

Since the popular verdict has long ago decided that *The Mikado* is on the whole "the best" of the Gilbert and Sullivan works, and since no critical opinion, whether dramatic or musical, disagrees very strongly with this idea, I feel justified in taking this libretto as being representative of Gilbert at his most characteristic. If this is granted, it clearly shows how small a part in his artistic make-up is taken by considered and deliberate satire. In most of his previous compositions—in all, indeed, except *Princess Ida*—the scene had been set specifically in England, and his plots were necessarily so full of mockery of specific English institutions, manners, customs and anomalies that it was often difficult to say for certain whether plot or satire came first.

In *The Mikado,* placed as it was in a mediaeval Japan which had never in fact existed, it seems to me that no such difficulty confronts us, and we can say with confidence that the plot comes first and is carefully planned, whereas the satirical content is incidental and even casual. G. K. Chesterton would not agree here, because he saw this opera as the most deliberate, mordant satire on England which Gilbert ever wrote. But Chesterton was apt to be too brilliant on occasion, and I think that he allowed himself, in this case, to be carried away by an attractive and ingenious argument.

He thought that the character of Pooh-Bah, the high-born noble who, when the cheap tailor Ko-Ko was elevated to the post of Lord High Executioner and all the great officers of State refused to serve under him, accepted all their posts (and their salaries), was a satire on English life. I find this impossible to accept. Chesterton's thesis is that in Gilbert's England there was a great deal of pluralism—that a man of social importance or outstanding ability might hold a number of appointments, and that these appointments might interlock so as to give him an undue share of influence. He might, for example, be a director of a company applying for a licence, and a member of the authority from which that licence must be obtained. So far, Chesterton is on safe ground; but when he goes on to imply that this kind of pluralism was specially characteristic of the England of Gilbert's day, he is in grave error. Nor has he any ground for the suggestion that pluralism is in itself wrong, or that Gilbert thought so.

The point about Pooh-Bah is not that he is a pluralist, but that he is a greedy and corrupt pluralist who operates on a ridiculous scale. He is a humorous rather than a satirical conception. We have seen already in more than one of the operas how Gilbert delighted in the notion that a man's duty in one capacity might conflict with his duty in another. In *The Pirates of Penzance,* Frederic's duty up to 12 o'clock was to serve the Pirate King, after that to destroy him. Patience was placed in a similar dilemma, so were several of the characters in *Ruddigore,* so especially was the Lord Chancellor in *Iolanthe.* Now in Pooh-Bah we have the same idea carried to its logical extreme in a character who, to mortify his proud spirit, accepts a large number of incompatible duties and carries out whichever best suits him at a given moment. The Lord High Everything Else could only be accepted as a satire on English life if England had happened at the time to be a mass of jobbery and corruption, or if Gilbert had happened to think it was. Neither was the case.

Again, Chesterton calls attention in another place to the flick of satire in the trio where Ko-Ko, Pitti-Sing and Pooh-Bah give their detailed but false account of the scene of Nanki-Poo's execution. After the first verse, the chorus gives its corroboration in these terms:

> We know him well,
> He cannot tell
> Untrue or groundless tales—
> He always tries
> To utter lies,
> And every time he fails.

This, says Chesterton, is written in mockery of the absurdly exaggerated Victorian belief that the upper classes were placed above the ordinary temptations that beset human nature and were therefore immune from them. That this belief existed is certainly true. I can myself remember hearing people expressing shocked surprise if it became known that " a man of that class " had done something mean or petty. They liked the aristocracy's sins; when it committed any, to be on a scale big enough to do it credit.

According to Chesterton, then, a correct interpretation of the chorus quoted above would be, " This is a man belonging to a class so exquisitely well-bred that even when he tries to tell lies he cannot bring it off." But this is manifest nonsense, because the man of whom the chorus is speaking is not " of that class " at all; it is Ko-Ko, the jumped-up tradesman with whom none of the nobles will condescend to associate. Chesterton, in fact, has been so deeply occupied in making a neat job of his argument that he has based it on the wrong facts.

In my view, Gilbert here, once again, is simply being humorous and has no satirical intent. The scheme of the lyric calls for three verses, each describing in vivid detail the death of a man who is actually alive and well, and for corroboration after each verse from the Chorus. Each of these corroborative choruses has to have in it a comic idea, an exaggeration or unexpected twist designed to get a laugh. In the first verse the laugh comes at the absurd picture of a man struggling constantly but in vain to be a liar, in the second at the idea of somebody whose " taste exact for faultless fact amounts to a disease," and in the third at the equivocal tribute to a person who " speaks the truth whenever he finds it pays." None of these corroborations is specially fitted to the character of the person on whose behalf it is uttered; with a few trifling verbal changes any of the choruses could follow any of the verses. The Chorus does not care what it says, for like the three principals it is telling lies anyway.

So far from being deeply satirical in intention, *The Mikado* is a straightforward piece of nonsensical story-telling, and is almost completely self-explanatory; and that, no doubt is why it was the only opera of the series to become widely known outside the English-speaking countries. Topical references to the contemporary scene are few, in spite of the fact that the opera takes its colour not from Japan but England. Nanki-Poo's opening song, " A Wandering Minstrel I," gives parodies of the kind of sentimental, nautical or patriotic ditties which were popular, and there are a few references to the manners and customs of Victorian England in the Mikado's song about letting the punishment fit the crime, and again in Ko-Ko's " I've Got a Little List "; but these, too, are self-explanatory.

Almost the only line of the opera which is meaningless without a footnote occurs half-way through the second act, when the Mikado reveals that the wandering minstrel Nanki-Poo is his son. He asks Ko-Ko to produce him:

Ko-Ko:　In point of fact, he's gone abroad.
Mikado:　Gone abroad?　His address!
Ko-Ko:　Knightsbridge.

Knightsbridge is the London street in which the Japanese Exhibition of 1885, already referred to, took place.

CHAPTER IX

"Ruddigore" and "The Yeomen of the Guard"

The Mikado ran for 672 performances, and long before it showed signs of flagging Gilbert had made his plans for its successor, and had secured Sullivan's approval. It seems that the magnificent success of *The Mikado* had modified Sullivan's dislike of supernatural or impossible elements, for the plot of the new piece had a good share of both. Perhaps, however, Sullivan accepted the idea of *Ruddigore, or The Witch's Curse,* merely because to have done otherwise would have involved him in another argument over the " lozenge " plot, which Gilbert still regarded with favour.

In this piece we find Gilbert once again pointing out the absurdities of an institution he loved—this time the theatre, for *Ruddigore* was burlesque melodrama. It was written, as to its dialogue, in an inflated old-fashioned idiom which Gilbert had several times used in all seriousness for his straight plays. Its central figure was Sir Despard Murgatroyd of Ruddigore, a wicked baronet; and not only he, but each of the other people of the play as well, is a caricature of a stock figure of the mid-Victorian stage. There is the pure young village maiden, Rose Maybud; the honest young farmer, Robin Oakapple; his faithful servant, Old Adam Goodheart; Richard Dauntless, a breezy sailor; and Mad Margaret, whom Gilbert describes in his stage-direction as " an obvious caricature of theatrical madness," Every one of these stage types would be instantly recognisable by a Victorian audience, and each would be expected to behave in character; and so they all do—but each one is given a Gilbertian twist.

119

Sir Despard, for instance, is a wicked baronet not only because of the Victorian stage convention that all baronets in melodrama are wicked, but also because of an ancient malediction by the terms of which the head of the house of Ruddigore must commit a crime a day, or die in hideous torment. In himself, he is a virtuous young man who tries to atone for his statutory crimes by doing good for the rest of the day. "Yesterday I robbed a bank and endowed a bishopric. To-day I carry off Rose Maybud, and atone with a cathedral."

Rose herself is so consciously the village belle that she actually introduces herself to a stranger as "sweet Rose Maybud." And to ensure propriety of behaviour on all occasions she carries a book of etiquette with her everywhere, and acts only on its instructions. In addition she contrives, under an appearance of sweet rustic innocence, to be a gold-digger of the most relentless description. Her lover, Robin, to outward view just a bashful village swain, is actually Ruthven Murgatroyd, Sir Despard's elder brother, who has changed his identity to avoid inheriting the family title and the curse that goes with it; and his bashfulness conceals not only a sublime conceit but a complete lack of sympathy with his brother's hard fate.

Richard Dauntless is the most subtle Gilbertian invention of them all. In manner and appearance he is the honest sailor, whose determination always to obey the dictates of his heart is obviously a credit to him because he is obviously good-hearted. In fact, however, his heart invariably exhorts him to act for his own selfish advantage. Having promised to woo Rose on behalf of the shy Robin, he takes her for himself without a twinge of conscience. He gives away the secret of Robin's identity to Sir Despard, so that Robin has to take over the curse and the baronetcy and become bad, and therefore no longer worthy of Rose. In fact, Richard's behaviour, always with the approbation of his convenient heart, is one long series of double-crosses.

The essence of Richard is shown in his song, " The Bold Mounseer." This is a parody of the sort of popular patriotic ballad in which one Englishman used to be represented as equal to half-a-dozen Frenchmen. A British revenue sloop sights a French merchantman and makes for her, but she turns out to be a well-armed frigate:

> Then our Captain he up and says, says he,
> " That chap we need not fear—
>   We can take her if we like
>   She is sartin for to strike,
>   For she's only a darned Mounseer,
>   D'ye see?
>   She's only a darned Mounseer.
> But to fight a French fal-lah—it's like hittin' of a gal—
>   It's a lubberly thing for to do;
>   For we, with all our faults,
>   Why, we're sturdy British salts,
>   While she's only a Parley-voo
>   D'ye see?
>   A miserable Parley-voo!"

With these noble sentiments on her Captain's lips, the British ship " has pity on the poor Parley-voo," and turns round and runs for her life!

The humour of this inversion appealed very much to English audiences, with their odd liking for running themselves down (one of the secrets of Gilbert's appeal to his countrymen is that he is constantly saying rude things about them, disguised as compliments.) Unfortunately, the French could not see the joke. They mistook the parody for just one more example of boasting patriotism, refused to listen to explanations, and were deeply offended.

As all the people of this story are caricatures, Gilbert is

121

constantly bringing out their disingenuousness by passing twists of plot and touches of dialogue. Robin Oakapple, for instance, says of himself, " Ah, you've no idea what a poor opinion I have of myself, and how little I deserve it." And Rose Maybud, having engaged herself to penniless Richard, shows immediate readiness to throw him over as soon as she finds that the wealthier Robin is in love with her too. It was a favourite trick of Gilbert's to make his characters conceal quite shocking behaviour under an appearance of bland virtue, and in *Ruddigore* he finds chance after chance to play it.

Exactly in tune with the spirit of deliberate stage caricature which pervades this opera is the chorus of professional bridesmaids. In the machine-made melodramas of his time Gilbert had seen so many village weddings attended by so many bevies of bridesmaids that it was a legitimate and telling stroke of burlesque to imagine a village in which the corps of bridesmaids is endowed by a pious charity, and goes on duty in the appropriate clothes every day from ten to four. This joke has lost most of its point with the passage of time, but there is still some amusement to be got from the use the author makes of his idea. The male chorus is given an extremely important and impressive share in the action. It appears in the second act as the ghosts of the dead-and-gone Murgatroyd ancestors, who step down from their frames in the Ruddigore picture-gallery to make sure that their latest descendant carries out the terms of the curse.

The denouement of the plot is contrived by one of Gilbert's own particular twists of chop-logic. Robin, as Sir Ruthven, proves quite unable to commit any really satisfactory crimes. Except that he has shot a fox—which is not against the law, but is nevertheless a fearful thing to do in a country addicted to fox-hunting—the Ghosts are not satisfied with him; and he resolves to defy them and die bravely rather than be a wicked baronet in good earnest. Then an idea strikes him. A Baronet of Ruddigore can only die by refusing to commit his daily crime; but to refuse to commit his crime is punishable by death, and amounts to suicide, which is itself a crime (a line of argument already glanced at in *The Mikado*). Therefore the previous holder of the title is logically not dead and can return to earth. Robin is a farmer again, and can marry Rose. Despard can settle down with Mad Margaret, who is now, except for lapses, a reasonable church-worker; and Richard's heart is satisfied with the leading bridesmaid.

Ruddigore does not quite establish itself among the best of the Gilbert and Sullivan operas, though it has never dropped out of the D'Oyly Carte Company's repertoire without being eventually restored. Its original run at the Savoy Theatre, which began on January 22nd, 1887, was 283 performances—better than that of *Princess Ida,* but less than half that of *The Mikado*. Its values are all stage values, and its satire has no relation to real life except at two removes. American playgoers who find its allusions or its atmosphere obscure might seek some kind of illumination by relating it to the old barn-storming melodramas of their own theatre of the same period. Such remarks as Sir Despard's " Ha! observed! And by a mariner!" or Robin's " Foiled—and by a Union Jack!" are obvious parodies of bad melodramatic writing of the period. We can no longer laugh at them with spontaneity, but we can recognise them in passing as humorous topical comments. Rose Maybud's errands of mercy in the village (with highly unsuitable gifts), and her way of offering a not very appetising apple to any character in distress, is a parody of the stock behaviour of the Pure Young Heroine; and the spirited fight in defence of her honour put up by the respectable Dame Hannah when she is carried off in the second act is a burlesque of a similar stock scene between Villain and Distressed Damsel.

Once its remoteness from real life is grasped, *Ruddigore* presents few difficulties to the modern playgoer. Indeed, in one respect it is the most modern of all the operas, for it is an example—perhaps the first example—of that game which has been in vogue on the London stage ever since 1930 or so, the game of guying the Victorians. It was a marked characteristic of playgoers " between the wars " that they had no great liking for or understanding of any straight play that was not strictly realistic. Consequently the Victorian play, and particularly the Victorian melodrama, seemed to them the most exquisitely foolish compositions that had ever been committed to paper by human hand. Somebody had the idea of staging these plays mock-seriously, and the joke caught on; and from that moment to the one at which I write these words, 20 years later, it has been almost true to say that no day has gone by on which no audience anywhere in London has been invited to laugh at the absurdity of the Victorian stage. To playgoers trained in this school, *Ruddigore* must be comprehensible to a degree that is actually disconcerting, offering as it does a proof that their fine new jest was being enjoyed by Gilbert many years before the oldest of them were born.

When the run of *Ruddigore* came to an end George Edwardes, the famous manager of the Gaiety Theatre, spoke of it as a failure. Gilbert's sharp retort was that he could do with a few more such failures as it had put £7,000 into his pocket, and Edwardes wished he had not spoken. All the same, Gilbert was not really satisfied by the public reaction to *Ruddigore*, and no doubt that is why, in choosing his next story, he acceded to Sullivan's desire for a plot that should owe nothing to magic or impossibility. *The Yeomen of the Guard* was, in fact, a straightforward piece of play-writing in comic-operatic form.

In this particular case, Gilbert has left it on record how the idea for the new work first came to him. A firm called the Tower Furnishing Company had issued an advertisement bearing a picture of one of the warders of the Tower of London, who still wear their picturesque ancient uniform, and are popularly known as " Beef-eaters." Gilbert saw this poster on a railway platform, and the thought struck him that the Tower would make an excellent setting, and the Beef-eaters themselves a most effective chorus, for the more romantic and realistic kind of " book " that he now wanted to write.

The Tower itself has always had a romantic appeal, ever since it ceased to play its day-to-day part in London's history and became a show-place for visitors. Built in the 11th century, after the Norman Conquest, it had steadily played its part, sometimes as fortress, sometimes as refuge, more often at a later date as political prison, for hundreds of years. It had been the scene of the death of many great historical figures, men and women, good and bad. It had atmosphere in every stone.

It was not Gilbert's purpose, however, to tie himself to any historical characters, or even too closely to any period. " Time—16th Century " is all the indication he gives, and this is useful merely to establish the costumes of the characters. His hero is not even a political prisoner, but a gallant young Colonel Fairfax who is awaiting execution on a charge of having had dealings with the Devil, trumped up by a cousin who inherits the Fairfax estates if the Colonel dies unmarried.

Considered as realism, this story is not very deeply convincing, and even less likely is the situation which develops from it. Fairfax is resigned to death, but has a natural wish to get even with his cousin by dying a married man; and he asks the Lieutenant of the Tower, an old friend of his, to find him a bride. The Lieutenant offers a hundred crowns to Elsie Maynard, a strolling player, if she will consent to be the blindfolded bride of a condemned prisoner. She consents.

It is strange that Gilbert did not see, or did not allow himself to be influenced by, the legal consequences of this. As soon as Elsie is Fairfax's wife she becomes entitled, not merely to the Lieutenant's bribe, but to her husband's estate. The fact that she does not know who her husband is has no validity, for unless the Colonel's widow can be produced and prove her title, the estates will still go to the wicked cousin. The secrecy which surrounds the wedding is therefore a mere theatrical trick, to bring it about that when Fairfax escapes death by disguising himself as a Tower warder, Elsie can fall in love with him without recognising him as her husband. Once this basic improbability is allowed, however, the plot moves forward smoothly enough, and enables Gilbert to turn the people of the story into real characters, not denizens of topsy-turvydom. For this reason, and because Sullivan welcomed the chance to prove that his serious music was better (as he thought) than his lighter compositions, *The Yeomen of the Guard* has a gravity unique in Savoy opera, and in the opinion of many admirers of Gilbert and Sullivan is their best work.

It was not so regarded by the public. It was staged at the Savoy on October 3rd, 1888, and ran for about a year. Its 423 performances put it fifth in order of length of run among the operas so far written—a betwixt-and-between position which was high enough to make Sullivan use it as an argument for writing more seriously still, and low enough to make Gilbert feel disinclined to repeat the experiment.

The cleavage of opinion between the two men on this point had already grown so wide as to jeopardise the partnership. Sullivan was still constantly being told, and still believed, that he was wasting time and the chance of a great reputation by continuing to write light music, and even the greater seriousness of *The Yeomen* did not content him. Indeed, after he had approved the story, and while Gilbert was at work on the text, Sullivan suddenly announced in a letter from Monte Carlo, that he was going to abandon comic opera. One of the reasons for this change of heart was the fact that a piece called *Dorothy*, by B. C. Stephenson and Alfred Cellier, was having an enormous success at the Gaiety Theatre. Cellier, who shared with his brother Francois the post of conductor at the Savoy, was a musician whom Sullivan considered much inferior to himself, and as the run of *Dorothy* went on and on (it ended by beating easily the longest of the Savoy runs, with 931 performances) the conviction grew in Sullivan's mind that it was beneath his dignity to continue to write popular music if others could be more popular still. This was a frame of mind with which Gilbert had no patience, and he managed—aided perhaps by Sullivan's bad luck at the tables—to persuade his partner to face the practical issue, that serious music would not enable a man to live in the extravagant style to which Sullivan had long been accustomed. And so *The Yeomen* was completed in due course, while D'Oyly Carte filled in time with successful revivals of *Pinafore* and *The Mikado*.

The title of the new piece gave Gilbert much trouble. *The Tower of London* was the first suggestion, followed at varying intervals by *The Tower Warder* and *The Beef-eater*. None of these was entirely satisfactory, and the author's relief was considerable when the much more attractive *The Yeomen of the Guard* occurred to him. The actual writing of the piece, however, went smoothly and gave him great pleasure. Sharing as he did Sullivan's desire to be known for more serious work, he revelled in the chances which this story gave him for the creation of character. There is more feeling in a page of *The Yeomen* than in the whole of any other libretto that Gilbert wrote. Phoebe Meryll, the gallant

127

little conspirator whose love for Fairfax has to be sacrificed, is one of the few among Gilbert's young women for whom it is possible to feel an affection; while Jack Point, the jester who must be funny though his heart is breaking, is the only character in the entire range of Gilbert's writings whom I feel he understood with his heart as well as his brain. It was Gilbert's great fault as a dramatist that when he aimed at sincerity he nearly always fell into sentimentality. For Jack Point, however, he had a fellow-feeling as a professional humorist, and it kept him straight.

Because *The Yeomen of the Guard* was not light entertainment but a play set to music, the text needs hardly any elucidation. There was little opportunity in such a piece for topical satire, which would make nonsense of a historical setting. In place, then, of the patter-song full of familiar allusions we have songs like " A private buffoon " or " The man who would woo a fair maid," which besides their particular appositeness to the situations at which they come in the play have some sort of general application outside it.

The language in which *The Yeomen* was written is the same stage " period " language in which we have seen Gilbert expressing himself before—the very same kind of language, in fact, which he had used with burlesque effect in *Ruddigore*. It serves its purpose well enough, but it is a curious mixture, varying from Jack Point, who uses a Shakespearean vocabulary, to Phoebe Meryll, whose idiom is that of Victoria England. But it needs no annotation, for its meaning is always entirely clear.

" I never knew
I was talking to
An influential fairy."
[Miss Louie Rene and Charles Workman as The
Fairy Queen and The Lord Chancellor in *Iolanthe*]

" Oh, why am I moody and sad?"
[Richard Watson as Sir Despard Murgatroyd in *Ruddigore*]

CHAPTER X

"The Gondoliers"

In the last chapter I made passing mention of the different reactions of author and composer to the run of *The Yeomen of the Guard*. Gilbert frankly confessed that he much preferred writing this kind of consistent story to wild fantasy, but he pointed out to Sullivan in a letter that the public had not really taken *The Yeomen* to their hearts and obviously preferred the fantasies. To go against their verdict and write something more serious still would be unwise, indeed dangerous.

Sullivan did not agree. For him, *The Yeomen* had been a belated step in the right direction, the direction in which his serious-minded musical friends, with a little powerful lay help from Queen Victoria, were constantly pointing the way— towards grand opera. He was determined to take the next step in that direction before it was too late, and in January, 1889, with the praises of *The Yeomen* still fresh in his ears, and with the piece going strong in the fourth month of its run, he announced to Gilbert that his next composition would not be light opera but something of much greater musical importance, and he asked Gilbert to write him a book. D'Oyly Carte had approved the scheme, and was building a big new opera house which he proposed to open with the new work, and then to run as a home of English opera.

Gilbert took time to think the proposition over, and then refused, good-temperedly enough. He did not think there was a public for English grand opera, he did not approve of the site of Carte's new theatre, and he did not feel that the book of a grand opera, in which the librettist has usually a very unimportant share, would give him any chance to do

E

good work. He sympathised with Sullivan's wish to work on a nobler scale, but suggested that there was no reason why he should not do both kinds of work. The letter reached Sulivan at a time when he was in no mood for any such compromise, and there was an exchange of increasingly heated letters in which Sullivan poured out, both to Gilbert and to Carte, a flood of grievances which had been accumulating for years. Gilbert, to his fury, found that Sullivan thought that he had been sacrificing himself to his partner all along the line, that his music was too good for the kind of work they were doing together, and that he was a deeply wronged man. Gilbert flung off the accusation. His practical theatre-sense told him that the strength of their work lay in the fact that neither had " sacrificed himself," and that in the ordinary give-and-take of collaboration he had always studied Sullivan's wishes. " If we meet," he said early in the controversy, " it must be as master and master." All through April, 1889, a battle of words went on, but with decreasing acrimony; and in May the two met in London and found that their open quarrel had once more cleared the air. It was by now settled between Carte and Sullivan that the new Royal English Opera House was to be opened in rather over a year's time with a serious opera for which Sullivan could choose both theme and librettist. Before he began work on this, therefore, he would be able and willing to write a lighter piece if Gilbert could produce a story that he liked.

Gilbert produced *The Gondoliers,* which Sullivan liked very much indeed. They set to work at once in an atmosphere of the greatest friendliness which was maintained throughout the writing of the piece. It was staged at the Savoy on December 7th, 1889, and at once took the place which it has kept ever since among the prime popular favourites of the Gilbert and Sullivan canon. It ran for 554 performances at its first production, and—owing perhaps to the increasing topicality of its theme—has retained its freshness longer than any other Savoy opera except *The Mikado*.

That theme is social and political equality—a subject on which humanity in general was beginning to have different views in Gilbert's day, and has been discussing those views with increasing vehemence ever since. This is the third highly controversial theme which he has taken for the plot of a libretto—the nature of art in *Patience* and the rights of women in *Princess Ida* are the others—and it is interesting to compare his handling of the three.

A controversial theme is one in which equally authoritative voices may be heard speaking with equal confidence in opposite senses, and on which, in consequence, the ordinary citizen with no special knowledge does not know what he ought to think. He finds himself as a rule alternating unhappily between the two extreme opinions and able to agree to some extent with both, and he longs to hear the detached voice of cool common-sense enunciating some more moderate opinion with which he can thankfully identify himself. Gilbert, as we have seen, was in the ordinary way common-sense personified. He was not a politician, not a doctrinaire, and on all subjects but one he was able to let his heart be ruled by his head. Thus, in *Patience,* he was able to point out to the playgoers of many successive generations that the object of our scorn should be, not the artist, but the pretentious charlatan masquerading as an artist. In *Princess Ida,* because his sentimentality about women clouded his vision, his common-sense failed him and the opera quickly lost its hold on the playgoer. But in *The Gondoliers* he is once again without prejudice, and he achieves such a miraculous quality of detachment that even after half-a-century and more of intensive social and political changes such as Gilbert himself would have considered revolutionary, what he has to say about equality still appeals to the plain man as plain sense.

At the time when *The Gondoliers* was written, Socialism, for most people, was just a notion which idealists talked about. The average citizen's view of it did not go much farther or deeper than that a few people like Bernard Shaw and H. G. Wells thought that all the money in the country ought to be shared out equally. Sometimes he read an article by Mr. Shaw or a story by Mr. Wells and realised that the Socialist idea was not quite so childishly crude as that, but he still had a feeling that their schemes, whatever they were, wouldn't work unless human nature were to undergo a change, which its whole history seemed to show was most unlikely.

In *The Gondoliers* Gilbert turned the lantern of his common-sense on the ideal of equality and examined it, as the Socialists usually omitted to do, in the light of human nature. He imagines a pair of gondoliers in 18th century Venice— partly with an eye to picturesque dresses and settings, but also because Venice, a historic republic, was likely to produce young men with strongly egalitarian principles. They are inseparable brothers, and have just married. Suddenly they learn that one of them (it is uncertain which, until an old lady in Spain can be consulted) is King of Barataria, and that it has been arranged that as that country is in a state of insurrection they shall reign jointly until it is known to which of them the crown belongs. What would happen, asks Gilbert, if they were to accept the situation, and put Socialist views on equality into operation?

It may be objected here, with perfect truth, that Gilbert nowhere uses the word " socialism "—that he is imagining, not a modern Socialist State with a planned economy, but simply an old-fashioned monarchy run oh exaggerated republican principles. The answer is that whatever Gilbert imagined himself to be doing, in fact he was not addressing his ridicule to the republican form of government but to doctrinaire egalitarians wherever they might be found. Also, the touch is feather-light. But the conclusion that Gilbert comes to, that men are not born equal, cannot be made so by governments, and do not really want to be so, is the clear voice of sense. Don Alhambra's song about the kind-hearted king who

> wished all men as rich as he,
> (And he was rich as rich could be),
> So to the top of every tree
> Promoted everybody

has more point now than when it was first written. It is more solidly based than any idealistic doctrine which takes no account of the differences between individuals.

Gilbert was so little of a politician, however, that having stated this devastating home-truth he makes no dramatic use of it. He is not really concerned to hammer home the lesson. Having brought Don Alhambra to his final pronouncement:

> In short, whoever you may be,
> With this conclusion you'll agree—
> When everyone is somebodee
> Then no-one's anybody,

he leaves the whole question of equality to settle itself, and turns to the more rewarding task of sorting out the matrimonial tangle of two husbands and three wives. Once again, he is humorist rather than satirist.

In general, the text of *The Gondoliers* needs little annotation. Except for the political issues so lightly touched on, it is nearly all concerned with love and laughter, and the excitement of the discovery that certain humble people may be, for all they know, kings and queens. There is little that can be called social criticism in Gilbert's handling of this part of his theme—so little, indeed, that Queen Victoria, who was apt to be exceedingly touchy about jokes of any kind at the expense of royalty, is reported to have laughed with real enjoyment at the song " Rising early in the morning," with its refrain:

> Oh, philosophers may sing
> Of the troubles of a king;
> Yet the duties are delightful and the privileges great;
> But the privilege and pleasure
> That we treasure beyond measure
> Is to run on little errands for the Ministers of State.

How she reacted to the other song about royalty, " A regular royal Queen," is not recorded. Her wrath might have been tremendous if she had taken to herself words such as:

> And noble lords will scrape and bow
> And double them into two
> And open their eyes
> In blank surprise
> At whatever she likes to do.
> And everybody will roundly vow
> She's fair as flowers in May
> And say, " How clever!"
> At whatsoever
> She condescends to say.

Perhaps, however, she saw that the joke was aimed not at queens but at sycophantic courtiers; if so, she may well have agreed with the sentiments expressed.

All the real social satire in *The Gondoliers* is centred upon the Duke and Duchess of Plaza-Toro. They represent a type comparatively rare in Gilbert's day, but grown increasingly familiar ever since—the poverty-stricken aristocrat who is prepared to sink his pride, and sell his aristocratic privileges for what they will fetch. We are apt now to look back on the late 19th century as a time when the leisured landed gentry of England were still paramount, but in fact the flow of the wealth of the country from them to the industrialists was in full spate. It was still thought degrading, however, for members of this class to enter industry themselves, or indeed to work at all except at certain accepted and usually ill-paid professions. Consequently quite a number of people began to find it impossible to keep up the appearance of leisured ease without additional income earned in the only way in which they could earn it—by capitalising their social position.

It was one of Gilbert's happiest and most characteristic strokes to imagine such a man capitalising his social position in good earnest, by turning himself into a public company. " I, the Queen of Barataria!" says Casilda, when the fact is announced to her. " But I've nothing to wear! We are practically penniless!" Here is her father's answer:

> That point has not escaped me. Although I am unhappily in straitened circumstances at present, my social influence is something enormous; and a Company, to be called the Duke of Plaza-Toro, Limited, is in course of formation to work me. An influential directorate has been secured, and I myself shall join the Board after allotment.

A truly Gilbertian flight of fancy, as unlikely ever to be realised as any that he made—yet in our time it has come true almost exactly. Many of our great landowners have turned themselves into companies—not their persons, admittedly, but their estates—in order to be assessed for taxation as business firms and so avoid the very high surtax levied on big private incomes.

To Gilbert, this practice would have seemed a very

delirium of dishonesty. He was no more a business man than he was a politician, and to him the whole principle of a limited liability company seemed little better than a legalised method by which swindlers could avoid paying their just debts. In *The Gondoliers* he does no more than glance at the subject and pass on; but we have already seen how often a casual reference in one opera gave him his main idea for the next, and so it was to prove here. The Duke of Plaza-Toro's ingenious scheme for restoring his fortunes gave Gilbert the whole plot for *Utopia Limited*. In its proper place, therefore, I shall return to this subject.

When the Duke and Duchess arrive in Barataria with their daughter Casilda the company has duly been floated and they are both splendidly dressed. The Duke announces himself in his new style as " The Duke of Plaza-Toro, Limited," and after a little time he and the Duchess explain in a long duet exactly what services they render to shareholders. In this song, much more than in most of his satirical lyrics, Gilbert really is driving straight at the side of human nature that he most deeply despised—its petty corruptibility, its readiness to indulge in intrigue for unworthy objects, its small-minded snobbery. This was why he disliked politicians, and though he neither knew nor cared much about politics, he regarded them all as actual or potential place-hunters. He himself was entirely free from this particular weakness. For instance, he was never jealous of Sullivan's knighthood, and felt no particular gratification about his own when it came; in fact, he only accepted it because up to that time nobody had been given a title simply for writing plays, and he thought it might be good for the profession.

Here, then, is the Duke's account of his own proceedings. He uses his social influence to procure small titles and orders for civic dignitaries—mayors, aldermen and recorders (a recorder is the chief legal official of a city); to get military rank conferred on people with no real right to it; and to get baronetcies for otherwise obscure Members of Parliament. He lays foundation-stones for a fee; he makes after-dinner speeches at dinners in aid of charity for a rake-off of 10 per cent. of the takings. He permits his name to be used as an advertisement by cheap tailors, though the clothes they make are so bad that Robinson Crusoe would not care to be seen in them, and he is a director of fraudulent companies. As for the Duchess, her activities are milder, though similar in kind. She launches ladies of doubtful reputation on society, lends her presence (at " five guineas a night and her dinner " plus her winnings at cards) to middle-class parties, recommends bad dressmakers, and writes puffs for patent medicines and complexion soaps. The song ends:

> In short, if you'd kindle
> The spark of a swindle,
>   Lure simpletons into your clutches,
> Or hoodwink a debtor
> You cannot do better
>   Than trot out a Duke or a Duchess.

There is no need to underline the searing cynicism of this; Gilbert so seldom went in for searing cynicism that it underlines itself. It stands right outside the mood of gentle mockery at the absurd ways of men in which *The Gondoliers* is written; it shows not amusement but indignation. To us to-day, indeed, that indignation seems overdone. We are so accustomed to seeing leading ladies of society—to say nothing of stage or screen—smiling at us from the advertisement pages of magazines that we forget how deeply shocking such a spectacle would have been in the 1890's. In those days there was still a large leisured class which abhorred personal publicity instead of courting it, and looked askance even at the famous society beauties like Lily Langtry who allowed their photographs to be sold in the shops. (In the end, Mrs. Langtry capitalised her charms by going on the stage, thus putting herself definitely outside the pale.)

To Gilbert, then, it was a dreadful sign of the decadent times that noblemen should be needy, or that, being needy, they should invent ways of getting money to keep up appearances. He would much have preferred them to bear their poverty proudly, even it they carried that pride to ridiculous lengths. I am told that there was in Spain, not so very long ago, the head of a great house so poor that his ancestral home was falling to pieces about him, and he and his ragged-liveried servants were all starving together; yet when an American engineer offered him a large sum of money for the right to carry a railway across his land he merely replied that it was beneath the dignity of a grandee of Spain to take part in commercial transactions. Gilbert, I feel, would have understood his attitude—indeed, he showed this clearly by mocking at its antithesis in Pooh-Bah; he did not at all understand that he was witnessing the first signs of a change in social values brought about by the shift of wealth away from the leisured classes, or that those classes would shortly lose most of their leisure and be compelled to look for work like the rest of the community.

What he saw was that a certain number of titled people, finding themselves for the first time in their lives in need of more money, and finding moreover, to their surprise and sometimes bewilderment, that City financiers were ready to pay them salaries as directors of companies merely in order to have their names on the board, accepted these appointments without making proper enquiries. At first these " guinea-pig " directors, moving as they were in an unknown world, sometimes found themselves involved in shady dealings through carelessness and ignorance. They soon learnt their lesson, however, and began to look with a suspicious eye on money that seemed too easy.

If Gilbert had been able to foresee that within 50 years this shift of wealth would have been so much accelerated by the impact of two great wars that many of the English landed gentry would be unable to live in their own homes any more, he might have abated his indignation in the song under notice, and the song itself might not to-day have seemed so out of touch with reality.

The only other lyric in the opera which depended for much of its effect upon contemporary allusions was the first-act duet by Marco and Guiseppe describing the egalitarian state they intend to set up in Barataria:

> For everyone who feels inclined
> Some post we undertake to find
> Congenial with his peace of mind—
> And all shall equal be.

Then follows a list of those who are to share in this cheerful levelling-up process. The first batch needs no comment:

> The Chancellor in his peruke—
> The Earl, the Marquis, and the Dook,
> The Groom, the Butler and the Cook—
> They all shall equal be.

The second, however, will be clearer for a little explanation:

> The Aristocrat who banks with Coutts,
> The Aristocrat who hunts and shoots,
> The Aristocrat who cleans the boots—
> They all shall equal be.

Banking with Coutts implies its own elucidation—that Coutts Bank was famous for the number of famous and titled clients whose names were on its books. The next line, just because it seems even simpler in the meaning that it conveys, is in fact much more complicated; for in this sentence the word " hunt " and the word " shoot " are used in highly specialised senses. Anybody who chases after any kind of animal at any time of year and with any kind of weapon may be said to hunt, just as anybody who uses any kind of gun at any target may be said to shoot. If, however, you were to ask a member of the English upper classes in Gilbert's day, " Do you hunt?" or " Do you shoot?" you would know quite well (and so would he) that you were not just enquiring whether he killed animals for food, or could hold a gun.

" Do you hunt?" to such a man would mean, " Do you as a regular habit, or whenever you get the chance, take part in a highly-organised piece of pageantry in which, at certain seasons of the year, certain animals, some edible like stags and hares, some inedible like foxes and otters, are chased with traditional ceremony by packs of specially-bred and highly-trained hounds? Are you prepared to go to immense trouble and to spend large sums of money over this exercise; and do you on the whole consider that people who do not do so are benighted beings, hardly worth your attention?"

In the same way, " Do you shoot?" would mean, " Is it your pleasure at certain well-defined times of the year, either on your own country estates or those of your friends, to take part in miniature but very carefully planned campaigns, designed to denude selected stretches of country of the chief forms of wild life there resident? Are you rich enough, and have you enough leisure, to spend a great deal of money and time on this elaborate way of performing a very simple act?"

Field sports have now been largely democratised, but in Gilbert's day they were almost a prerogative of the owners of the great estates now broken up. And so " the Aristocrat who hunts and shoots " has to be understood as meaning quite a considerable aristocrat.

CHAPTER XI

"Utopia Limited"

Hardly had *The Gondoliers* settled into its steady stride than a quarrel broke out between the three partners in the Savoy management, compared with which all previous disagreements seemed like lovers' tiffs. So far as anybody but the participants knew at the time it was Gilbert who began the quarrel by making too much of a trivial grievance; but it seems now that the fault really lay with D'Oyly Carte.

The correspondence between the partners has not survived, but Hesketh Pearson in his book *Gilbert and Sullivan* produces a piece of evidence which, though not first-hand, is credible and significant. Jack Robertson, an old actor of the Savoy company, told Mr. Pearson that Gilbert had shown him an unforgivably offensive letter from Carte, in the light of which all Gilbert's subsequent conduct must be judged. Assuming that this letter was as Robertson described it, here is the sequence of events.

The agreement between Gilbert, Sullivan and Carte was that each should pay an equal share of the production expenses for each opera. When the bill for *The Gondoliers* was presented Gilbert found it unexpectedly heavy and, asking for details, found that Carte had included £500 for new carpets for the auditorium. Gilbert wrote to Carte in some annoyance, the gist of his argument being that the carpets did not properly come under the head of production expenses and that he should have been consulted before they were bought. In reply to this (so Robertson said) Carte wrote to say " that both Sullivan and himself were tired of the perpetual interference of Gilbert in matters that did not concern him, and that if this kind of thing continued he (Carte) and Sullivan would have to look for another librettist.''

Taking this letter as a basis, Pearson very plausibly suggests that Carte had fallen into the common error of under-rating Gilbert's importance to the collaboration. No librettist in theatrical history had ever taken the lead as Gilbert took it, and Carte's belief in Sullivan—proved by his readiness to pour out money over Sullivan's grand opera—may well have caused him to share Sullivan's feeling that Gilbert must be kept in order. If so, Carte and Sullivan were in for an exceedingly rude awakening.

Gilbert was deeply offended, as might have been expected. He was the best theatre man of the three, and he knew it if the other two did not. So did the Savoy company, who were solidly on Gilbert's side in the quarrel that followed. Sullivan was at Monte Carlo when it began, but when he returned he was in a difficulty, because he could not afford to lose Carte's goodwill. He took a middle course. Gilbert found this as infuriating as Carte's rudeness, and declared the partnership at an end. Subsequent interviews did no good. Gilbert's sense of injury made him even more touchy than usual. He lost his temper royally and finally brought a lawsuit against the other two for money due to him, won it, and felt better. Like most hot-tempered men after a battle of words, he was now rather surprised to find that the things he had said in the heat of the fray had caused wounds which did not heal immediately. However, by November, 1890, some sort of peace was patched up.

Now came a series of unpleasant surprises for Carte. On January 31st, 1891, his magnificent new theatre, the Royal English Opera House, was opened with Sullivan's grand opera *Ivanhoe*. The venture and the work were given a tremendous send-off by the critics and by society. Queen Victoria expressed her personal approbation, and claimed a share in the credit for the opera's existence. But the general public did not care much for Sullivan in his heroic mood, and the run of the piece only amounted to 160 performances in spite of the most lavish production; and Carte, losing faith in English grand opera, sold the theatre—now the Palace—to a music-hall syndicate. Sullivan, deeply disappointed, realised that his real genius was, after all, for the lighter kind of music and began to look out for a librettist who should be a more amenable Gilbert.

Meanwhile, Gilbert himself had found a composer in Alfred Cellier, of *Dorothy* fame, who was ready to handle the lozenge plot which Sullivan had refused. The lozenge had become a liquid by the time the libretto was finished, but the idea was the same as before, and *The Mountebanks,* produced at the Lyric Theatre on January 4th, 1892, was quite a success and ran for 229 performances. Then, later in the same year, on September 24th, Sullivan's new light opera, *Haddon Hall,* written by the fashionable dramatist, Sydney Grundy, was staged at the Savoy by D'Oyly Carte and also had a fairly good run of 204 performances—though one gathers that the piece was often played to empty houses and did not rank as much better than a failure.

Carte had to face the plain fact that by insulting Gilbert he had done himself a very bad turn indeed. Sullivan was not better without Gilbert after all—in fact the librettist was doing rather better without the composer than the composer without the librettist. It was plain, however, that neither was his full self without the other, and by the end of 1892 the three partners had come together again and Gilbert set to work on the book of *Utopia Limited,* or *The Flowers of Progress.* It was produced at the Savoy on October 7th, 1893.

At the time of its first appearance, *Utopia* was ranked among the great Gilbert and Sullivan successes. This may seem a very strange saying to modern playgoers who have hardly even heard of it, but it is true. The critic of *The Times* ranked it firmly above *The Gondoliers*, for he said that the collaborators had done nothing so good since *The Mikado*. Later commentators, writing about the opera more coolly, have not assessed it quite so high as that, but they have treated the work, particularly Gilbert's share of it, with marked respect. Gilbert at his best, a fair summing-up of their opinion might run, and Sullivan not much below his. And yet, popular taste has never agreed with their verdict. The opera's first run finished after 245 performances, which was noticeably better than *The Mountebanks* or *Haddon Hall*, but only just as good as *Princess Ida* and not as good as *Ruddigore*. And unlike the last two, it has never been professionally revived in London. Its music is not generally known. None of the excellent numbers with which it is said to abound is ever played by the bands in the parks, or by orchestras on the radio. To the best of my knowledge, I have never heard a bar of the music Sullivan wrote for it, though Gilbert's libretto, having been printed in his collected works, is as familiar to me as any of the others.* There seems to be no logical reason why so good an opera should have been so very markedly neglected, and I am led to the conclusions that a number of causes, none of them sufficient in itself, had enough combined weight to thrust *Utopia* into an oblivion it does not deserve.

One suggested cause is that here, for the first and only time, Gilbert delivered an open, frontal attack on English manners, customs and traditions. Utopia, in the opera, is far from being the civilised State imagined in 1516 by Sir Thomas Moore when he invented the name; it is more like

---

* Since these words were written I have heard and seen this opera, privately performed by the Gilbert and Sullivan Society. I found the music effective but disappointingly obvious, and came away with no very strong desire to hear any of it again.

the land of the lotus-eaters, where men lay under the trees
and let the fruit drop into their mouths. Gilbert imagines
it as a semi-barbaric kingdom somewhere in the Southern
Seas, whose king, fired by admiration of England, sends his
eldest daughter to Girton (one of those women's colleges at
which Gilbert had poked fun already in *Princess Ida*) so that
on her return she can remodel his State on the English
pattern. This certainly does give Gilbert the chance to be
more direct in his satire than before, but I do not believe that
the public found anything offensive in that. The English
never mind being laughed at so long as there is kindness or
tolerance in the laughter, and Gilbert had long enjoyed the
same licence to say what he liked as was given to Bernard
Shaw by a later generation. Laugh as he might at the things
in his country's ways that he considered absurd, Gilbert was
intensely loyal and intensely English, and his public knew it.

A second suggestion, which I think has rather more
importance than the other, was that the popularity of the
piece was affected by the offence taken to it by Queen
Victoria's court. One of the first reforms put into practice
by Princess Zara on her return to Utopia is to hold a
Drawing-Room copied, with improvements, from the London
original. Court procedure was closely imitated, and the
dowdiness and austerity of Victoria's State functions were
pointed out in passing. Zara, for instance, decides to have
her Drawing-Room in the evening instead of Victoria's
afternoon hour, because " we all look so much better by
candlelight "—a consideration which did not weigh with the
grim ideas of court etiquette which the English Queen had
absorbed from her German husband. And after the function
is over, two of the six so-called Flowers of Progress—English
officials whom Zara has imported to show the Utopians how
things are done—have a short self-congratulatory chat:

Lord Dramaleigh:	Well, what do you think of our first South Pacific Drawing-Room? Allowing for a slight difficulty with the trains and a little want of familiarity with the use of the rouge-pot, it was, on the whole, a meritorious affair?
Mr. Goldbury:	My dear Dramaleigh, it redounds infinitely to your credit.
Lord D.:	One or two judicious innovations, I think?
Goldbury:	Admirable. The cup of tea and the plate of mixed biscuits were a cheap and effective inspiration.
Lord D.:	Yes—my idea, entirely. Never been done before.

The court did not like this at all, for with the steadily growing democratisation of old aristocratic traditions and the gradual loss of privilege, London society was at this time very much on its dignity for fear it should soon have no dignity left. It liked even less another passage, which to the modern reader means very little but to the contemporary mind was very pungent criticism. King Paramount of Utopia, about to hold its first Cabinet council, asks Lord Dramaleigh, as Lord Chamberlain, to arrange the formalities. He makes the Ministers bring up chairs so that they are sitting in a semi-circle across the stage with King Paramount in the middle, Lord Dramaleigh on his left and Mr. Goldbury on his right. The outer chairs are occupied by Captain Fitzbattleaxe (Army), Captain Sir Edward Corcoran (Navy), who is apparently Ralph Rackstraw of *H.M.S. Pinafore* grown middle-aged, Mr. Blushington (a County Councillor) and Sir Bailey Barre (an eminent lawyer):

King:	Like this?
Lord D.:	Like this.

King: We take your word for it that this is all right. You are not making fun of us? This is in accordance with the practice at the Court of St. James's?

Lord D.: Well, it is in accordance with the practice at the Court of St. James's Hall.

King: Oh! It seems odd, but never mind.

The King then sings a patter-song, with chorus, about the reforms which the English Cabinet has introduced, after which all the chairs are replaced, and the stage left clear.

All this was taken by the Court as a deep and deliberate insult to the Queen and her Ministers. The point is that a popular entertainment of the day, which held its place for so many years at St. James's Hall in Piccadilly that it seemed one of London's permanent institutions, was given by the famous Christy Minstrels, who during the first part of their performance always sat round the stage on a semi-circle of chairs and joined in the refrains while one of their number sang a solo; and that the production of King Paramount's song imitated that of the Minstrels very closely. I doubt whether Gilbert meant anything but a cheerful flick of irreverence such as Englishmen have always allowed themselves about their kings, but society was shocked, and decided that he was implying that a beloved Queen and her noble Government were no better than a set of black-face comedians. We hear of a sort of half-hearted boycott of *Utopia* by the court, and this may have had some effect in restricting its original run, though I find this hard to believe with any real seriousness. The number of people who would have refrained from visiting the Savoy because the court considered it not " the thing " must have been more than balanced by those who want to see for themselves what the fuss was about, even in those solemn days; as is shown by a report current at the time that no member of the

Queen's entourage would go to see the offensive thing—more than once.

My own belief is that the opera had a comparatively short original run not so much because it offended patriotic prejudice or court sense of decorum, but chiefly because in this piece, for once in a way, Gilbert subordinated his great skill as a humorous story-teller and concentrated on satire; and there never has been in the English theatre a very big public for satire, as such. Satire, to the average English playgoer's taste, may be a good servant but is certainly a bad master. This kind of playgoer goes to the theatre to be told a story, preferably romantic. While he is held by that story he is prepared to accept with pleasure any incidental entertainment that he may be offered. But if the story fails to hold him, and he is thrown back on to the incidental entertainment for his evening's enjoyment, he is bored. A quick glance at the plots of the operas already dealt with will show that in practically all of them there is a romantic story in which boy (the principal tenor) gets girl (the leading soprano) at or near the fall of the curtain.

In *Utopia Limited* there is no such romantic story, for boy (if I may so refer to Captain Fitzbattleaxe of the First Life Guards) has already got girl (with all respect to the Princess Zara) when they arrive on the stage, and nothing whatever occurs during the whole action of the piece to sunder the lovers, except when the Princess's court train arrives from the dressmaker and she wants to try it on. True, there is a passing mild threat of trouble in store when the two all-powerful Wise Men fall in love with the Princess; but Gilbert handles it in very perfunctory style and the threat never materialises. This is not the kind of thing that attracts the average playgoer, and the wonder really is that without any real love interest the piece ran as long as it did.

The same reason may well account for the fact that this opera has never been revived; but I believe that there are other reasons, equally important. Nothing loses its point so quickly as satire which is mainly topical in its impact, and *Utopia Limited* was not merely topical but local. We have seen that *Patience* has owed its long life to the accident that its satire applies not merely to the aesthetes of Gilbert's day, but to all artistic poseurs of any time or country. This is not true of *Utopia*. The satire there is addressed to the special absurdities of the late Victorian era in Britain, and has hardly any validity outside that time and that place.

Also, *Utopia Limited* has the disadvantage, which it shares only with *Princess Ida*, that it is not rooted in Gilbert's superb common-sense. *Princess Ida*, as we have seen, grew from his belief that the higher education of women is an absurdity, and has languished because general opinion does not support his belief. In the same way, general opinion fails to agree with his contention that the idea of a limited liability company is absurd, or that it is an invitation to fraud. And since it was out of this contention that *Utopia* grew, this opera also is withered at the root.

It would be interesting to know just why Gilbert fell foul of the Joint Stock Company Act of 1862 at this particular period in his life, more than a quarter of a century after the Act had become law. It was his way, as this survey of his work has shown, to keep on hammering away at anomalies; but his first mention of limited liability is in *The Gondoliers* when the Duke of Plaza-Toro capitalises his social prestige by registering himself as a company under the Act. My suggestion—which is only a guess—is that Gilbert, not being in any sense a business man, had never had any clear notion what a limited liability company was until his happy thought in *The Gondoliers* made it necessary for him to look it up. Having looked it up, and having perhaps a layman's instinctive distrust of financial experts, he set himself, if not to laugh the Act out of existence, at least to warn

the investing public of the risks it was running. But the
investing public, seeing that the Act worked fairly well
however bad it might be, was not impressed.

Here is the song in which Gilbert epitomised his feelings.
It is put into the mouth of Mr. Goldbury, the company
promoter whom Princess Zara has imported to be Comptroller
of the Utopian Household:

Some seven men form an Association
    (If possible, all Peers and Baronets),
They start off with a public declaration
    To what extent they mean to pay their debts.
That's called their Capital: if they are wary
    They will not quote it at a sum immense.
The figure's immaterial—it may vary
    From eighteen million down to eighteenpence.
        I should put it rather low;
        The good sense of doing so
    Will be evident at once to any debtor,
        When it's left to you to say
        What amount you mean to pay
    Why, the lower you can put it at, the better.

They then proceed to trade with all who'll trust 'em,
    Quite irrespective of their capital
(It's shady, but it's sanctified by custom);
    Bank, Railway, Loan or Panama Canal,
You can't embark on trading too tremendous—
    It's strictly fair, and based on common-sense—
If you succeed your profits are studendous—
    And if you fail, pop goes your eighteenpence.
        Make the money-spinner spin!
        For you only stand to win
    And you'll never with dishonesty be twitted.

> For nobody can know
> To a million or so
> To what extent your capital's committed.

> If you come to grief, and creditors are craving,
>   (For nothing that is planned by mortal head
> Is certain in this Vale of Sorrow—saving
>   That one's Liability is Limited)
> Do you suppose that signifies perdition?
>   If so, you're but a monetary dunce—
> You merely file a Winding-up Petition,
>   And start another Company at once!
>   Though a Rothschild you may be
>   In your own capacity
>   As a Company you've come to utter sorrow—
>   But the Liquidators say
>   "Never mind—you needn't pay,"
>   And you start another Company to-morrow.

On the conclusion of this lyric King Paramount remarks in recitative:

> Well, at first sight it strikes us as dishonest,
> But if it's good enough for virtuous England—
> The first commercial country in the world—
> It's good enough for us . . .

And he decides then and there to turn Utopia into a limited liability company.

I have quoted this song in full, both because it is the core of the opera's plot, and because it sheds a double light on its author. It illustrates Gilbert's extraordinary faculty for making a clear statement in light verse, and it shows what a propensity he had, when his customary detachment was disturbed by prejudice, for overstating a case. The song is quite a fair statement of the way in which a fraudulent financier might keep his shady doings within the law, but it is completely unfair in its insinuation that all joint-stock concerns are " shady, but sanctified by custom." Gilbert makes it seem, indeed, as if the introduction of limited liability had made the way easy for fraud, whereas the fact is that the heyday of fraudulent finance came before the Act was passed.

Apart from conjecture, however, there is one purely practical reason why the D'Oyly Carte organisation may well have fought shy of reviving *Utopia*. It has always been an extremely expensive piece to produce, for the uniforms and court dresses in the second act must be genuinely impressive or their significance is lost. Sullivan was appalled at the estimated expenses of the original Savoy production, which must have been a mere fraction of what it would cost to-day. For this reason, if no other, we may never see this opera restored to the repertory—though it is possible that in these days, when people tend to look on the Victorian times as a huge joke, this contemporary lampoon might gain a new appeal.

I have said already that one of the most fascinating points about Gilbert's technique, for anyone who cares about such things, is the quickness with which he starts his libretti moving. *Utopia Limited* is an excellent example. Before he can proceed to satirise England, he has to make his audience familiar with the very peculiar methods by which Utopia is being governed—" a Despotism tempered by Dynamite." King Paramount is not so paramount as he sounds, for though technically an autocrat he is in fact at the orders of two Wise Men, who will have him blown to pieces by the Public Exploder if he disobeys them. This rather far-fetched notion is put across smoothly and amusingly in the shortest possible time, together with the King's admiration of English ways and customs. And then, with the entry of the two younger princesses, twins of 15 years of age, the criticism of those ways and customs begins.

Unlike their elder sister Zara, these two girls have never been out of Utopia; but they have been specially trained by their English governess, Lady Sophy, to be the very pattern of what a governess would wish a Victorian young lady to be. They are quite inhumanly good, demure, modest and cold; and the King, as they explain in their opening song, wants all Utopia to profit by their example:

> To please papa, who argues thus—
> All girls should mould themselves on us
>> Because we are
>> By furlongs far
>>> The best of all the bunch—
> We show ourselves to loud applause
> From ten to four without a pause—
> Which is an awkward time because
>> It cuts into our lunch.

Gilbert had not only ideas but ideals about women, but they did not include approval of mock-modesty. He had a bitter dislike of the old-fashioned code of manners inculcated by Lady Sophy, and he makes unmerciful fun of it not only in the young Princesses' own song but in the scene following, in which the governess uses her pupils as exhibits in a lecture on how a modest young English lady should receive the advances of a pushing young man. At the end of this, before she marches the twins away, she has two lines of recitative:

> The lecture's ended. In ten minutes' space
> 'Twill be repeated in the market-place.

I referred above to Lady Sophy's code as "old-fashioned," and it is a fact that by 1893 there was a discernible movement towards freedom and naturalness among women. Gilbert's clear common-sense was always apt to be clouded by romanticism where women were concerned, and he failed to see that it was woman's wider education (at which he still lost no chance of sneering) that was giving her the desire and confidence to be natural (at which he was delighted). But however illogically he came to his opinion, he left nobody who saw or read *Utopia Limited* in any doubt what that opinion was. For in the second act the twins try their demure ways on Lord Dramaleigh and Mr. Goldbury, and learn (to their almost incredulous delight) that the highest type of English girl is not a bit like that. Mr. Goldbury fairly lets himself go about her. " She is frank, open-hearted and fearless, and never shown in so favourable a light as when she gives her own blameless impulses full play.'' Prose is inadequate to express his feelings, and he bursts into song:

A wonderful joy our eyes to bless,
In her magnificent comeliness,
Is an English girl of eleven stone two
And five foot ten in her dancing shoe.
　　She follows the hounds, and on she pounds—
　　The " field '' tails off and the muffs diminish—
Over the hedges and brooks she bounds
　　Straight as a crow from first to finish . . .

There is a good deal more about her prowess on the playing-field and on the ballroom floor, and then:

Her soul is sweet as the ocean air,
For prudery knows no haven there;
To find mock-modesty, please apply
To the conscious blush and the downcast eye.
　　Rich in the things contentment brings,
　　　　In every pure enjoyment wealthy,
　　Blithe as a beautiful bird she sings,
　　　　For body and mind are hale and healthy.

Her eyes they thrill with right goodwill—
    Her heart is light as a floating feather—
As pure and bright as the mountain rill
    That leaps and laughs in the Highland heather.

Here, in the midst of his most satirical piece, is the clearest expression of the Gilbert who was a sentimentalist about women. This picture of what was then called " the outdoor girl " is done with such naive enthusiasm that for us it produces a first reaction almost opposite to what the writer intended. Surely, we think, Gilbert is laughing at her—such a very large young woman! And then we remember that in those days large young women were the fashion; we realise that Goldbury (and Gilbert) means every word to be taken as serious praise, and we try to dismiss the mental image of a red-faced Amazon thundering along on a cavalry charger. After all, it took courage and character in those days to shake free of the Lady Sophys; and if Gilbert felt that to meet a girl with natural manners was like a breath of fresh air, that was because she was still a rarity in Victorian London.

It can be seen from the extracts already quoted that Gilbert follows in *Utopia Limited* his usual method of assuming a thing to be right while it proves itself wrong. Mr. Goldbury describes his financial methods, and the audience see him as a scoundrel. The twin Princesses make themselves out to be paragons, and we perceive that they are minxes.

We might have expected the author to let the plot of *Utopia Limited* develop on similar lines—and so he does, but with a slight difference. Laugh as he might at the way in which the England of his day was run, he had to admit that on the whole she was run successfully; and therefore he could not plausibly hand over Utopia to the six Flowers of

Progress and allow them to fall short of successful government—or the critics would have been down on him at once, and with good reason.

Accordingly, he does once again what he had done so many times and so expertly before—turn the whole affair upside down. He makes the Utopians rise in revolt, not because they are being misruled but because they are being ruled too well. Each of the Flowers of Progress has contributed to this; Captain Fitzbattleaxe and Captain Corcoran have remodelled the Army and Navy so well that all their opponents have disarmed and war is impossible; the County Councillor's sanitary laws have put the doctors out of business; Sir Bailey Barre's new code has extinguished crime and litigation—Utopia is so prosperous that she is bored to death.

The King turns to his daughter, who is puzzled. England is not in this dreadful condition of dull perfection— she must have left some ingredient out. Sir Bailey Barre prompts her and she realises what that ingredient is—government by party:

> Introduce that great and glorious element—at once the bulwark and foundation of England's greatness —and all will be well! No political measures will endure, because one Party will assuredly undo all that the other Party has done; and while grouse is to be shot, and foxes worried to death, the legislative action of the country will be at a standstill. Then there will be sickness in plenty, endless lawsuits, crowded jails, interminable confusion in the Army and Navy, and, in short, general and unexampled prosperity.

If anything were needed to show that Gilbert was no politician, this speech would do it. By underlining the absurdities of party rule, he is saying, in effect, that the only sensible way to prosperity is a one-party government. If he could see the results of such rule in Europe to-day, he would have to admit that Zara's topsy-turvy speech has played Gilbert's own trick on its inventor, and has proved to be right way up after all.

From the very nature of its theme, *Utopia Limited* abounds in casual references to social and political matters, some of which I have been able to deal with in passing. Curiously enough, not very much is made in the end of the idea of a kingdom run on company lines, though the King uses it ingeniously to free himself of the two tyrannical Wise Men. He points out to them that as he is now no longer an individual but a company he is no longer in danger from the Public Exploder. You can't blow up a company, you can only wind it up. Like all Gilbertian characters, the Wise Men know irrefutable logic when they hear it, and admit defeat. Of another idea, however—the grafting of English customs on to the Utopian way of life—much more is made.

If my chief concern in this book were to develop the theme that Gilbert was no true satirist, I should find my best proof here. A true satirist in Gilbert's situation would be concerned to make his imaginary country a caricature, properly proportioned and consistent within itself, of the real country whose absurdities he is concerned to point out. Swift did this in *Gulliver's Travels*, Samuel Butler in *Erewhon*, Anatole France in *Penguin Island*. Gilbert makes no real attempt to do it in *Utopia Limited*, for he constantly turns aside to indulge either his sense of the ridiculous or his sense of the theatre.

Let me give examples of Gilbert in all three manners. He is being truly satirical when he mentions the fact that an English tenor named Wilkinson is appearing at the Utopian opera-house, and then allows it to turn out that the tenor is in fact not English at all, but a native Utopian who has taken an English name because (to quote King Paramount), " Bless you, they wouldn't listen to any tenor who didn't call himself English.'' This is a direct hit at the English opera-goers of Gilbert's time, who had it so firmly fixed in their heads that only foreign musicians were worth hearing that almost all English musicians were compelled to take foreign names before they could make a living.

Gilbert is allowing his sense of the ridiculous to get the upper hand in passages where the Flowers of Progress, taking advantage of the islanders' lack of knowledge of English customs, make them do things which are absurd in themselves—for instance, the arrangement of the Cabinet meeting in the form of a Christy Minstrel show, already described.

Finally, Gilbert is allowing his sense of the theatre to get the better of him in the scene where the Princess Zara and Captain Fitzbattleaxe, on finding that both the Wise Men, Scapho and Phantis, are in love with Zara, invent a stratagem to get themselves out of the difficulty. Here is the passage:

Zara: (*aside*) Oh, dear Captain Fitzbattleaxe, what is to be done?

Fitz.: (*aside*) Leave it to me—I'll manage it. (*Aloud*) Why not settle it in the English fashion?

Scapho and Phantis: The English fashion? What is that?

Fitz.: It's very simple. In England, when two gentlemen are in love with the same lady, and until it is settled which gentleman is to blow out the brains of the other, it is provided, by the Rival Admirers' Clauses Consolidation Act, that the lady shall be entrusted to an officer of Household Cavalry as stake-holder, who is bound to hand her over to the survivor in a good condition of substantial and decorative repair.

Sca.: Reasonable wear and tear and damages by fire excepted?

Fitz.: Exactly.

This precious scheme is accepted by the Wise Men, and as neither of the two cares to risk his life in the cause of love, the Princess remains under Captain Fitzbattleaxe's loving care for the remainder of the piece.

The whole scene is excellent Gilbert; but I hardly need point out that as satire it does not exist.

CHAPTER XII

How Long?

With *Utopia Limited* the Gilbert and Sullivan partnership really ended. There was in fact one more opera, *The Grand Duke,* or *The Statutory Duel,* which came to the Savoy Theatre on March 7th, 1896, and ran for 123 performances. Any piece which scores more than a hundred is usually entitled to be reckoned a success, but *The Grand Duke* was carried so far only by the impetus of the names on its title-page, and was an undeniable failure. It was a perfunctory piece of work by both collaborators, and on Gilbert's part was an attempt to carry to success the plot which had failed in the very first libretto which Sullivan had ever set for him. In *Thespis,* a company of strolling players take over the government of Olympus; in *The Grand Duke,* similarly, a theatrical troupe assumes the government of a small European state. This was never much of an idea, and I feel convinced that Gilbert came back to it merely because D'Oyly Carte called on him and Sullivan to fulfil their agreement. It was the last time, for all three of them.

The structure which Gilbert erected on this insecure foundation was characteristic enough in design but much too complicated. The Grand Duke of Pfennig-Halbpfennig, by a mixture of meanness and standoffishness, has infuriated his subjects till they have formed a conspiracy to dethrone him and instal the local theatre manager in his place. The secret sign by which the conspirators recognise one another is the eating of a sausage-roll—a clumsy device, which not only makes them all bilious but eventually gives away the plot to the Grand Duke's detective. At this point, very conveniently, a lawyer who is in the plot remembers an old law against

" I have a song to sing O."
[Henry Lytton as Jack Point in *Yeomen of the Guard*.]

" If ever, ever, ever
They get back to Spain
They will never, never, never
Cross the sea again."
[Martyn Green as the Duke, Ella Halman as the Duchess,
Margaret Mitchell as Casilda their daughter in *The Gondoliers*]

duelling, still valid but due to expire next day. By this law, disputes were to be settled not with weapons but by the drawing of a card; the man who drew the lower card was presumed to be dead, and the " survivor " took over his estate and his responsibilities. Let the manager and his leading comedian Ludwig fight such a duel, suggests the lawyer, and let the winner denounce the loser to the Duke as the leader of the conspiracy. Then the Duke will be satisfied, and the " dead " man can come to life again next day when the law expires.

This is far-fetched enough, but worse follows; for when Ludwig, having won his " duel," approaches the Duke to denounce the conspiracy, he finds that the Duke, too, is in such matrimonial difficulties that he would like to put an end to his existence if he could find a painless method. Ludwig sees his chance, proposes another statutory duel in which, by arrangement, the Duke draws a king and himself an ace. Ludwig thus becomes Duke—but only for a day, till the law expires, and the Duke can take over again with his difficulties solved. Ludwig's first act as Duke, however, is to renew the law for another hundred years, and so make himself permanent ruler of the duchy—or so he thinks, till Gilbert produces yet another twist. The law lays down, it now turns out, that when cards are drawn in a statutory duel, the ace always counts as the lowest card. This reverses the situation, and brings down the curtain.

It would be absurd to deny that *The Grand Duke* has merit. Some of the lyrics are as ingenious as anything in the operas. But it lacks life, and that indefinable air of plausibility which Gilbert, at his best, was able to infuse into the most unlikely situations. As a result, the piece is nothing better than a mechanical exhibition of the well-known Gilbertian bag of tricks. Also—possibly because the plot is so complicated that there is no room in it for running commentary on life—it adds nothing at all to the picture which I have been trying to build up in the minds of my readers of the world in which, and of which, Gilbert wrote.

It is the picture of an England serene in its present and secure concerning its future, an England whose problems were of policy, not of survival, an England rather too complacent in outlook, too ponderous in thought, too pompous in manner, and needing to be reminded from time to time to laugh at itself. But all Gilbert's career goes to show that it was an England ready to take such reminders in good part. That the Victorians were comic is a belief to which we who are their sons, grandsons and great-grandsons have long since persuaded ourselves, and we have spent so much of our time laughing at them with a kind of good-natured contempt that the joke is wearing thin. Gilbert laughed at them too, but he knew them better and his laughter was not contemptuous. That is why it will outlive ours.

What, now, are Gilbert's prospects of further life? Can he last much longer, now that he is in one way so out of date that books like this of mine have to be written to intepret him to his admirers? I have confessed in my opening chapter how wrong I was when once before I attempted to prophesy on this matter. If I now make a new prophecy in a sense completely opposite to that one, shall I be wrong again? I cannot say, and no more can anybody else. I will content myself, therefore, with a statement of the evidence for survival.

In general, it may be said that there are only two qualities which enable a dramatic author's work to be put before the public after his immediate vogue is over— universality and stageworthiness. Unless he has both of these, no dramatist can have anything to say to audiences of any but his own time.

How Long ?

About Gilbert's claim to universality there is very wide room for debate, for in his straight plays this was a quality which he conspicuously lacked. The faculty which a serious dramatist must have if his work is to be understood outside his own time and place is character-drawing, the ability to create men and women as they are, and not simply according to the theatrical fashions of his own day. Gilbert was more completely devoid of this faculty than seems possible in a man who took himself so seriously. The originality which he showed in the invention of his plots deserted him when it came to working out those plots in terms of character. He peopled them for the most part with lifeless puppets, made to the conventional patterns of a bad dramatic period.

In his work as librettist, however, the faults that had killed him as dramatist no longer got in his way. Plays written to be set to music cannot of their very nature go deeply into character, and as for stage conventions, there were none—or none that he did not brush aside at once. Here he was like a civilised conqueror taking over a backward country and giving it a new set of enlightened laws. So complete were these laws that his successors have had the greatest difficulty in adding anything significant to them. Even the best and most original librettists of succeeding generations constantly ran the risk of being accused of imitating Gilbert, and that of itself is a proof that in this particular branch of writing he had achieved universality.

In order to be universal, a writer does not need to be profound; what he does need is to be in his depth, and for the shallow waters of comic opera Gilbert was splendidly equipped. His detachment, his common-sense and his comic genius enabled him to create characters which, though not in themselves alive, were superbly recognisable travesties of life. And because they still are recognisable—because we can still meet people in ordinary life who remind us of Pooh-

Bah or Reginald Bunthorne, a generation for whom much of Gilbert's writing has become meaningless can nevertheless enjoy *The Mikado* and *Patience*.

As to stageworthiness, there is less room for argument. All through this book I have been hammering away at the point that among the chief assets owned by the unique Gilbert-Sullivan-Carte partnership was Gilbert's matchless theatre sense. Even when he is writing far below his best, that sense never deserts him; he is always actable. But " stageworthiness," in the sense in which I am using it here, is not simply actability. It is actability with something else added, and that something else is the response of an audience.

It is a matter of ordinary observation, as well as of theatrical history, that the tastes of audiences change very rapidly from generation to generation as well as vary sharply from country to country and from town to town, and that the change is most rapid and the variation sharpest in the field of comedy. One man's joke, notoriously, is another man's emetic; and on that reckoning we must not be surprised if Gilbert's hold on the public gradually slackens and finally fails, till at last he has to be pronounced no longer stageworthy.

Or is there, perhaps, a kind of comedy which remains perpetually stageworthy—which is in fact universal? I remember a conversation I once had with one of the leading London " comics " of his day after he had been out on the road for six months with a highly successful farce. " There are about two hundred good laughs in that play," he said, " but there weren't more than a dozen of them that were absolutely sure-fire. A line that was good for a round of applause in Birmingham might fall absolutely flat in Manchester; while as for Aberdeen . . . !'' He went on to develop a clown's philosophy of laughter, which I have never forgotten and have never had to modify.

Laughs in the theatre, he said, are of three kinds. There is the line-laugh, which depends on a twist of dialogue. This is the trickiest kind of laugh, and you can never be sure of it. A line which has been received with a roar at every performance of a London run is found to have no point for provincial audiences, just as a line which has gone over big in London is received in New York with a puzzled silence— and vice versa.

Then there is the character-laugh—the line which is not necessarily funny in itself but becomes funny because it shows up some quality in the mind or person of the character who speaks it. (For an obvious instance of this kind of laugh, we can take the remark in *Iolanthe* made by the Fairy Queen about Strephon: " I see no objection to stoutness, in moderation." The words in themselves have no comic force at all—they are funny only because a large lady says them.) This kind of laugh, my friend said, is a great deal safer than the line-laugh, but still is not really safe. A quick audience will laugh at many small strokes of character which a sluggish audience, or one not familiar with the circumstances, will miss. For example, a London audience at a play about an American small town, or a New York audience at an English rustic comedy, cannot be expected to recognise more than a proportion of the quirks of local character on which the author relies for his laughs.

Last, there is the situation-laugh. In this category come the only sure-fire laughs, valid at all times and in all places. The situation-laugh differs from the other two because it has no intellectual pretensions—it is purely theatrical, arising out of the thing done rather than the thing said. It is, as a rule, quite irresistible. When a pompous character in a farce sits down by accident on his very expensive hat, the laugh that goes up is free of all barriers of time, space, colour, creed or taste. Everybody laughs; or at least anybody who doesn't feel inclined to ought to be ashamed of himself, for his sense of propriety is out of order.

Applying this clown's philosophy to Gilbert, we find him pretty well versed in all three methods of exciting laughter. Witty and apposite lines flowed from his pen, and he had in private life a reputation for quick repartee that has endured to this day. Many of these lines—as I have had occasion to point out—are now no longer comprehensible, and the style in which they are written is no longer in much favour. Still, a reasonable proportion of them are still stageworthy. Character-laughs in a kind of writing not profoundly concerned with character-drawing, are naturally not so common, but they are very surely handled. Gilbert's favourite way of getting a character-laugh was by inversion and surprise; by making a character turn out the opposite of what is expected—as when a judge confesses himself a jilt, or a pirate is too tender-hearted, or a dairy-maid talks like a high-bred lady. Laughs of this sort do not suffer much by the passage of time, they remain fresh and funny.

But dozens of dramatic authors have equalled Gilbert in the ability to point a comic line, and hundreds have excelled him in the sense of comic characterisation. It is in his ability to invent comic situations that he stands alone—so much alone that anybody who attempts to join him on his own ground still is told at once, by critics and public alike, that he is a trespasser. The Gilbertian situation—an absurd state of affairs arrived at by logical argument—was something quite new when its author invented it, and has defied successful imitation ever since. It is here, surely, that the secret of his long hold on the public lies, and here that we must look if we want to guess at his chance of a further lease of immortality.

We need take only the quickest and most cursory glance back into theatrical history to see that the comedies which hold the most surely are the comedies with a well-knit bony structure of situation beneath their surface qualities. All the great Shakespearean comedies have it, and it is because *The School for Scandal* and *The Rivals* and *She Stoops to Conquer* are strong in this way that Sheridan and Goldsmith still succeed in our theatres when men of their time who thought themselves better dramatists are mere names in students' text-books.

From this point of view, it seems unlikely that a generation of playgoers will soon rise to which the predicaments of Ko-Ko and Nanki-Poo, Iolanthe and Strephon and the Lord Chancellor, Casilda or Josephine or Frederic will not seem to be funny.

In my first chapter, I pictured Gilbert's ghost in surprise that the frail-looking edifice which he and Sullivan enacted together has borne the stress of time so well. Now that I have come to my last paragraph I think he may not be surprised any longer. He may be proud to know that the building has lasted because it was founded on the living rock of his sense of situation.